Francis Abdelmassieh

Egyptian-Islamic Views on the Comparison of Religions

Beiträge zur Missionswissenschaft / Interkulturellen Theologie

herausgegeben von

Dieter Becker und Henning Wrogemann

Band 49

LIT

Francis Abdelmassieh

Egyptian-Islamic Views on the Comparison of Religions

Positions of Al-Azhar University Scholars on Muslim-Christian Relations

LIT

Cover image: Francis Abdelmassieh

This book is printed on acid-free paper.

Bibliographic information published by the Deutsche Nationalbibliothek
The Deutsche Nationalbibliothek lists this publication in the Deutsche Nationalbibliografie; detailed bibliographic data are available in the Internet at http://dnb.dnb.de.

ISBN 978-3-643-91280-0 (pb)
ISBN 978-3-643-96280-5 (PDF)
Zugl.: Wuppertal, Univ., Diss., 2020

A catalogue record for this book is available from the British Library.

Flössergasse 10
CH-8001 Zürich
Tel. +41 (0) 76-632 84 35
E-Mail: zuerich@lit-verlag.ch http://www.lit-verlag.ch
Distribution:
In the UK: Global Book Marketing, e-mail: mo@centralbooks.com
In North America: Independent Publishers Group, e-mail: orders@ipgbook.com
In Germany: LIT Verlag Fresnostr. 2, D-48159 Münster
Tel. +49 (0) 2 51-620 32 22, Fax +49 (0) 2 51-922 60 99, e-mail: vertrieb@lit-verlag.de
e-books are available at www.litwebshop.de

Preface

This book was accepted by the Bergische Universität Wuppertal in the spring of 2020 as a dissertation in fulfilment of the requirements for the degree of Doctor of Philosophy. It addresses an important topic in the field of Christian-Islamic relations, in which I served as a pastor of the Evangelical Presbyterian Church of Egypt for a total of thirteen years. My service in general and this research project in particular were governed by a constant effort on my part to contribute to understanding and peaceful coexistence among adherents of different religions, both on a practical and on a scientific level.

The success of this research project is due in large part to the support of a great many people. I am indebted to all of them. Unfortunately, I can name only a few at this point. First and foremost, I would like to thank my family – my wife, Evet, and our sons, Matthew and Calvin. After moving to Germany and being confronted with many new challenges in the first years, they always supported me with patience and cheerfulness, even and especially when I needed to devote a great deal of time to academic work.

I am particularly grateful to my PhD supervisor, Prof. Dr. Henning Wrogemann, for challenging, motivating, and guiding me. He also served as the first assessor of my writing. I learned much from him and alongside him. He devoted his time to me, kept on encouraging me, accompanied me on a study trip to Egypt, and opened up new ways of thinking for me. I would like to thank Prof. Dr. Dieter Vieweger in his capacity as second assessor, as well as Prof. Dr. Martin Ohst and private lecturer Dr. Thomas Wagner for serving on the examination board.

Then I would like to extend my sincere gratitude to prominent representatives of Al-Azhar University and to the leaders of various church bodies and seminaries in Egypt, especially those of the Coptic Orthodox Church, the Roman Catholic Church, and the Evangelical Presbyterian Church. They all opened their doors to me, welcomed me with great hospitality, and provided frank answers to my questions.

I would like to address a special word of thanks to Prof. Dr. Tharwat Kades. His help and his extensive network of relationships and friendships put me in touch with people actively involved in Christian-Islamic relations. Without him, many things would not have been possible. His great experience in Christian-Islamic relations in Egypt and his commitment to dialogue between German and Egyptian roleplayers really helped me shed light on this area from different angles.

In addition, I would like to thank the Friedrich-Ebert-Stiftung for supporting me with a doctoral scholarship for several years. Ms. Kathrein Hölscher and Ms. Barbara Nauruth deserve special mention for always helping me in such a friendly and reliable manner whenever I had questions. I am indebted to the Friedrich-Ebert-Stiftung for a generous printing subsidy towards the publication of this book.

Furthermore, I would like to thank the German Society for Missiology (DGMW) for financially supporting this book.

My hope is that this book will help identify issues in the field of Christian-Islamic relations in need of ongoing attention. Christians and Muslims believe in very different ways that God is one. In future, much will therefore depend on adherents of different faiths recognizing these differences equitably and candidly. In the same way, ongoing differences in the areas of faith, practice, and the image of God need to be borne in an attitude of tolerance.

Francis Abdelmassieh
Hermannsburg, March 2020

Contents

1. Introduction

In almost all countries of the world, religious actors play a significant role in civil society, and Egypt is no exception. In Egyptian society, al-Azhar University is the most important institution representing the Muslim side, whereas the Coptic Orthodox Church is the most important body on the Christian side. On both sides, scholars of religion are regarded as authorities speaking either for the majority Muslim population or the Christian churches as representatives of Egyptian Christians. But how do scholars of each religion view the religious heritage of the respective Other theologically? How do Christian theologians assess Muslim traditions – and vice versa? This study will explore the writings of several Muslim scholars who either were trained or are employed by al-Azhar. The focus of the study will be to analyze their approach and methodology as they engage in the comparison of religions. Since these scholars are responsible for training large numbers of students for work in various Egyptian state institutions and private organizations, it is evident that the way in which they approach and engage in the comparison of religions carries great weight. That being said, it is also difficult to measure.

This study is premised upon the conviction that a willingness to acknowledge the other religion within its own context is a necessary prerequisite for a comparison of religions to contribute to a better understanding and more peaceful relations between adherents of different religions. In order to explore the field of the comparison of religions and to assess the respective underlying theology of religion, it is important to focus not only on those scholars who share one's own point of view, but also and especially on those scholars who can be said to represent mainstream thinking. In other words, one should concentrate not on the very few thinkers considered by Europeans to be willing and able to dialogue, but on those scholars whom Europeans might well label "apologetic" in the polemical sense. In my observations as a native Egyptian, the latter represent the majority of scholars of religion at al-Azhar and beyond, and for this reason they also deserve far more consideration than is customarily given to them in European contexts. The real issues in Muslim-Christian relations come to the fore only if one is willing to recognize that these scholars play a seminal role even in today's Egyptian society. This study therefore aims to analyze how several well-known al-Azhar scholars approach and undertake the comparison of religions. Let us begin by setting the stage and providing general information on Egyptian society, past and present, and on its various social and religious actors.

1.1. Christians and Muslims in Egypt – a Brief Overview

In the centuries immediately following the Christ event, Christianity spread all over Egypt. It is said that the bishopric in Alexandria was founded by Mark, disciple of Christ and author of the Gospel of Mark. In addition to Constantinople, Rome, and Jerusalem, Alexandria was also a seat one of the four patriarchs of the ancient church. Famous Alexandrian theologians include Clement of Alexandria, Origen, and Cyril of Alexandria. Within a few centuries of the birth of Christ, the majority of Egyptians were Christian. In 642, however, Egypt was conquered by Muslim troops and remained under Muslim rule until the end of the 19th century.[1]

Over the centuries, the percentage of Christians in Egypt declined. This was due to the regulations of sharia law and to especially its provisions on family and inheritance law, since Christian men were not allowed to marry Muslim women, whereas Muslim men were allowed to marry Christian women under the constraint that their children become and remain Muslims. Under the rule of the Fatimid dynasty (968-1171), Christians were oppressed for a time; the situation grew worse under the dynasty of the Ayyubids (1171-1250), the reign of the Mamluk dynasty (1250-1517), and the rise of the Ottoman empire (16th-18th centuries).[2]

In the 19th century, significant changes took place under the rule of Muḥammad ʻAlī (1805-1848), his son Saʻīd (1854-1863), and his grandson Ismāʻīl (1863-1879).[3] Egypt became a nation state. Its rulers undertook land reforms, monopolized the country's resources, and, from the 1820s onwards, introduced various kinds of industry (especially the production of cotton), schools, academies, army training, legal reforms, print media, and other reforms as well. Non-Muslims were granted more rights than ever before. In 1855,

> the jizyah, a special tax on non-Muslims, was lifted and the Copts were no longer excluded from military service. In many areas, the Copts were placed on the same level as the Muslims. They served on Egypt's appointed and elected representative body from the time that the first consultative council was established in 1866, and frequently reached high office.[4]

[1] Peter E. Makari, *Conflict and Cooperation: Christian-Muslim Relations in Contemporary Egypt*. Syracuse: Syracuse University Press, 2007, 36-66.

[2] Makari, *Conflict and Cooperation*, 46-48.

[3] Alexander Schölch, "Der arabische Osten im neunzehnten Jahrhundert 1800-1914," in Ulrich Haarmann and Heinz Halm, eds., *Geschichte der arabischen Welt*, 5th ed. (Munich: Beck, 2004), 365-431; Mohammed Abū-Nimer, "Interfaith Dialogue in Egypt: National Unity and Tolerance," in id., *Unity in Diversity: Interfaith Dialogue in the Middle East* (Washington, DC: United States Institute of Peace Press, 2007), 143-153.

[4] Milad Iskander, "The Coptic Struggle after the Revolution of 1952," in Martyn Thomas, Adly A. Youssef, Heinz Gstrein, and Paul Meinrad Strässle, eds., *Copts in Egypt: A Christian Minority under Siege* (Zurich: G2W-Verlag, 2006), 37.

This was a crucial step towards the equality of all citizens. It was intensified by the Hamayouni Decree, a law which continues to be in effect today. Makari observes:

> Enacted during Sa'id Pasha's rule in 1856, the law reflected the movement to legislate equality among peoples, revoking any sort of discrimination based upon ethnicity, race, or religion. This law was in response to inequality that existed between the Muslim and non-Muslim communities. With respect to these communities, the decree reestablished Coptic personal status independence from the implementation of *sharia*; allowed for the formation of councils that would have sole responsibility for church financial matters and be allowed to discuss personal status matters; provided a process for requests to be presented by the pope to the sultan for church building and repair (this process has recently been changed by President Hosni Mubarak); allowed for the freedom to express and practice one's faith; made discrimination in hiring illegal; ended the exclusion of non-Muslims from the military; and legislated inclusive religious languages in the legal codes... Clearly, this law has important implications for the legal relationship between Muslims and non-Muslims. The fact that this decree is still a basis for religious tolerance and mutual acceptance is evidence of the transcendent principles it represented.[5]

Following the enactment of the Hamayouni Decree, the status of non-Muslims in Egypt improved significantly.

After a national bankruptcy in the 1870s, Egypt came under the financial control of European powers. In 1882, British troops occupied the country. During the period of occupation, the British "cut down the role of the Copts in order to gain the support of the Muslim majority."[6] Nevertheless, from the 1920s until the year 1952, Copts continued to be represented in the Senate, holding about 10 percent of the seats. But things changed dramatically following the 1952 revolution of Egyptian army officer Jamāl 'Abd al-Nāṣīr, known in English-speaking circles as Gamal Abdel Nasser (1918-1970).

1.2. Contexts of Egyptian Society since the Mid-20th Century

We need briefly to devote our attention to the overarching political trends and courses of actions of various Egyptian régimes since the mid-20th century in order to provide an overview of how various factors have influenced Christian-Muslim relations during this period. Such factors include the political agendas of different

[5] Makari, *Conflict & Cooperation*, 49.

[6] Iskander, *Coptic Struggle*, 37.

rulers (a nationalistic ideology, Arabic socialism, and an emphasis on Islamic heritage or on civil society), religious movements which arose (Muslim and Christian revival movements, Islamic militancy, and others), particular incidents which took place (signings of peace treaties, terrorist attacks, revolutions, and others), legal reforms (especially of Egyptian constitutional law), and the advent of new forms of media (such as satellite television, the internet, and social media) in the Arab world. This overview is not intended to be exhaustive; instead, we will proceed by way of example. Even so, it is important to consider these trends, incidents, and changes in order to understand the multiple influences and contexts which shaped and continue to shape Christian-Muslim relations in Egypt and other parts of the world today.

1.2.1. The Era of Jamāl ʻAbd al-Nāṣīr (1952-1970)

When al-Nāṣīr came to power in 1952, he took control of various institutions and spheres of Egyptian society, subordinating them to the state. During the rule of al-Nāṣīr, al-Azhar was nationalized, the Muslim Brotherhood was oppressed, and the Christian minority was largely excluded from the political arena. Al-Nāṣīr established an authoritarian régime with a one-party system which he propped up by granting a privileged status to the army as the backbone of his rule. He founded state-led mass organizations, created a large bureaucratic sector, introduced the censorship of newspapers and other media, supported the propagation of the ideology of Arabic socialism, and used the Egyptian secret service to silence his opponents. Massive land reforms were undertaken in order to break the power of wealthy landlords in the form of both private persons and religious endowments – Muslim and Christian alike. Al-Nāṣīr nationalized the bank sector, trade, and industries, and he took control of unions and of the umbrella organizations of journalists, doctors, students, engineers, and others.[7] Makari summarizes al-Nāṣīr's views on religion as follows: "Nasir thought that religion, if practiced in a way that neither interfered with other people's freedom nor obstructed the progress of the nation, was a positive element of a person's character. He denounced reactionary religion as a hindrance to the national project."[8] The reign of al-Nāṣīr was predominantly secular. Following the defeat of Arab troops by Israel in the war of 1967, religious sentiments arose and some militant religious groups were founded. This may be seen as the consequence of the commonly-held Egyptian view that they had been defeated by Israel because of a lack of (Muslim) faith on their own part. Others argued that the defeat was caused by dissatisfaction with the rule of al-Nāṣīr. After al-Nāṣīr died in 1970, his successor, Vice-President as-Sādāt, took over the presidency immediately.

---

[7] Gudrun Krämer, "Die Islamische Welt im 20. Jahrhundert," in Albrecht Noth and Jürgen Paul, eds., *Der islamische Orient: Grundzüge seiner Geschichte* (Würzburg: Ergon, 1998), 475-479.

[8] Makari, *Conflict & Cooperation*, 55.

1.2.2. The Era of Anwar as-Sādāt (1970-1981)

Anwar as-Sādāt (1918-1981) took a different stand to his predecessor in political and religious matters. On the one hand, he opened the country to foreign investment (mainly from the West) and introduced a multi-party system. In terms of foreign policy, he maintained a close relationship to the United States and later even took part in the peace process between Israel and the Palestinians (the negotiations held at Camp David in 1979). On the other hand, he left sectors like the state bureaucracy, the army, the police, the secret service, and the national party untouched. Later on in his presidency, as-Sādāt began to emphasize Islamic values more and more. By that time, the process of the Islamization of society had intensified significantly, being promoted among others by the Muslim Brotherhood. "While making frequent rhetorical reference to Egypt's pharaonic history to stress the common history of Muslim and Christian Egyptians, his presidency was a time during which sectarian conflict was fostered."[9] The president not only allowed the founding of different religious groups, but he also tried to legitimize himself in the eyes of the population by presenting himself on television as a pious Muslim, partaking in Friday prayers and the like.

Early on in his presidency, as-Sādāt altered the constitution of Egypt, inserting a phrase describing the *sharia* as *one* source of Egyptian legislation. In 1979, he changed the wording again to state that the *sharia* is the *principal source* of its legislation. Nevertheless, the question remained open as to what this phrase was supposed mean exactly. Nathan Brown observes:

> At its most ambitious, it seemed to incorporate the Islamic sharia into the constitutional order itself, requiring that ordinary legislation be drawn from, and be fully compliant with, the sharia. ... But far more modest readings of the provision were also possible – that it was merely a statement of fact or a vague directive to parliamentarians to consult the Islamic legal heritage for undefined "principles" as part of the legislative process. And nowhere did the article make clear how it could be enforced or was even meant to be enforced.[10]

Be that as it may, one obvious motive behind the change of the constitution was the effort to appease Islamists.

The 1970s saw a wave of re-Islamization in Egyptian society. It must be said that the policy of as-Sādāt opened up spaces not only for Islamist groups, but also for popular preachers like *Muḥammad Mitwalli al-Sha'arawi* and *'Abd al-Hamid Kishk*, whose influence steadily grew through media like radio, cassettes, and television.[11] Without doubt, such trends of the Islamization of the public sphere contributed to rising tensions between the different religious camps.

---

[9] Makari, *Conflict & Cooperation*, 56.

[10] Nathan J. Brown, "Islam in Egypt's Cacophonous Constitutional Order," in Said Amir Arjomand and Nathan J. Brown, eds., *The Rule of Law, Islam, and Constitutional Politics in Egypt and Iran* (New York: State University of New York Press, 2013), 236-237.

[11] See Aaron Rock-Singer, "Censoring the Kishkophone: Religion and State Power in Mubarak's Egypt," *The International Journal of Middle East Studies* 49 (2017): 437-456;

During the 1970s, not only were a number of radical Muslim groups like *al-Takfir wa'l-Hijra* founded, but more and more attacks on churches were carried out, with more and more Christians being killed. Makari states:

> It is ironic that many of the extremist Muslims, whom Sadat allowed to be openly expressive of their political and social views, accused the régime of favoring Christians and accused Christians of being in league with the administration and the Israeli Jews, with whom Sadat eventually signed the Camp David accords.[12]

In reaction to these accusations, as-Sādāt himself blamed the Coptic Orthodox Church and especially Pope Shenouda IV of destabilizing the country, since Copts had demonstrated in various different ways against as-Sādāt changing the constitution again. As-Sādāt finally exiled Pope Shenouda IV to a monastery. From 1980 to 1981, clashes, demonstrations, killings, and mass arrests took place. In 1981, as-Sādāt was assassinated by Khalid al-Istambuli, a member of the militant group *Islamic Jihad*.[13]

1.2.3. The Era of Ḥosnī Mubārak (1981-2011)

From early on in his presidency, Ḥosnī Mubārak had to come to terms with militant Islamism. While he maintained the policy of opening the country to foreign investment and opening public space to different media, at the same time, Mubārak repressed radial Islamist groups. In 1984, he released Pope Shenouda IV from exile. Mubārak allowed different parties to participate in elections, and even the Muslim Brotherhood was allowed to engage politically. While the first years of his presidency proved to be rather peaceful, tensions flared again significantly by the end of the 1980s. When in 1991 a group called *al-Jama'a al-Islamiyya* (the Islamic Group) took the Imbaba area in Cairo under their control and declared it to be an Islamic state, Mubārak sent the military and thousands of police officers to reconquer the area. In the meantime, the Islamists had already introduced several practices in the area, such as the *jizya*. According to traditional sharia law, the *jizya* is a special tax imposed upon non-Muslims – in this case, the *jizya* was to be paid by Christian inhabitants of the area in question.

---

id., "The Salafi Mystique: The Rise of Gender Segregation in 1970s Egypt," *Islamic Law and Society* 23 (2016): 279-305; id., "A Pious Public: Islamic Magazines and Revival in Egypt, 1976-1981," *The British Journal of Middle Eastern Studies* 42 (2015): 427-46; Jakob Skovgaard-Petersen, "Islamic Fundamentalism in Arab Television: Islamism and Salafism in Competition," in Ulrika Mårtensson, ed., *Fundamentalism in the Modern World: Fundamentalism and Communication; Culture, Media and the Public Sphere* (London: Tauris, 2011), 264-291; Charles Hirschkind, "Cassette Ethics: Public Piety and Popular Media in Egypt," in Birgit Meyer and Annelies Moors, eds., *Religion, Media, and the Public Sphere* (Bloomington, IN: Indiana University Press, 2006), 29-51.

[12] Makari, *Conflict & Cooperation*, 56.

[13] Makari, *Conflict & Cooperation*, 55-58.

Over the following decades, a number of violent incidents occurred, such as the bombing of churches, the killing of tourists, and other horrific events. The government tried to maintain its influence by way of a double strategy – asserting itself as legitimately Islamic on the one hand, while repressing radical groups on the other. Mubārak also tried to strengthen the sense of national unity. In 2002, he decreed January 7 (Coptic Christmas) to be a national holiday. At the same time, he supported al-Azhar and attempted to use it as a means to propagate a moderate version of Islam as "official Islam." With the liberalization of television, more and more religious programs began to be broadcast. In the late 1990s, a weekly television show was hosted by the grand imam of al-Azhar, Sheikh Muḥammad Sayyid Tantawi, representing a kind of moderate Islam.[14] In everyday life, moderate popular preachers like Muḥammad Mitwallī al-Sha'arāwī (1911-1998) continued to influence a broad variety of listeners in public spaces like restaurants or barbershops through programs broadcast on radio or television. The Islamic religious discourse therefore focused more on Islamic values in daily life and less on an Islamic political agenda, more on lifestyle and on improving one's own life circumstances and less on agitating against imaginary enemies, be they foreign powers or the government itself.

Furthermore, the Mubārak régime defied radical Islamist voices by citing popular preachers in support of Mubārak's rule – preachers like 'Abd al-Ḥamīd Kishk (1933-1999), who (like al-Sha'arāwī) was an alumnus of al-Azhar. Since Kishk was critical towards the government, the régime published or broadcast *censored* versions of his sermons. Responsible for the censorship were in particular the Ministry of Culture's (MOC) Censorship Board (*Jihaz al-Riqaba 'ala al-muṣannafāt al-Faniyya* in Arabic) and the Islamic Research Academy's Administration of Research, Composition, and Translation (*Idarat al-Buhuth wa-Ta'lif wa-l-Tarjama* in Arabic) of al-Azhar as well as the High Council for Journalism (*al-Majlis al-A'la li-l-Sihafa* in Arabic), founded in 1975.[15] Rock-Singer states:

> Claims to the reign of *ṭaghūṭ* – and associated understandings of divine sovereignty (*ḥākimiyyat allāh*), the just ruler (*al-imām al-'ādil*), and injustice (*ẓulm*) – had persisted in radical intellectual circles, including in 'Abd al-Salam Faraj's 1980 *al-Jihad: al-Farida al-Gha'iba* (*Jihad: The Hidden Duty*), and the blind shaykh 'Umar 'Abd al-Rahman's 1984 *Kalimat al-Haqq* (*The Word of Truth*). With the Mubarak régime facing a homegrown radical movement that considered both state and society to be un-Islamic, the MOC under the direction of Mubarak sought to reshape a key Islamist voice [the voice of *Kishk*], and the categories of political legitimacy on which he drew, in order to disarm this ideological movement.[16]

In this setting, Mubārak also made use of al-Azhar University in a particular way. Rock-Singer observes:

---

[14] Makari, *Conflict & Cooperation*, 67-90.

[15] Rock-Singer, *Kishkophone*, 438, 441.

[16] Rock-Singer, *Kishkophone*, 444.

> Just as the Mubarak régime has successfully regulated elements of the religious discourse within Egypt, it has also solidified the régime's religious legitimacy through the continued development of a professional religious class. This base includes professional preachers, teachers and government functionaries who have been trained at al-Azhar University and employed in government ministries such as those of Justice, Religious Endowments and Education."[17]

In other words: Despite the fact that society was comprised of two large bodies of religious adherents, Mubārak promoted moderate Islam by allowing moderate voices to appear in the sphere of the media and by employing especially alumni of al-Azhar University in posts within the state administration.

1.2.4. The "Arab Spring" (2011) and the Rule of ʿAbdel Fattāḥ as-Sīsi (2014-)

The protests in Cairo's Tahrir Square led to the end of Ḥosnī Mubārak's presidency and to parliamentary elections in November 2011. In January 2012, Muḥammad Mursī (also known in English-speaking circles as Mohamed Morsi) was elected president, but after additional protests, he was removed in 2013. In January 2014, a new constitution was adopted, and in May 2014, former general ʿAbdel Fattāḥ as-Sīsi was elected president. Since 2014, as-Sīsi has been trying to revive the tourism industry and to keep the peace by putting radical Islamist groups under state control or putting their activists in custody. Concerning the relation of Christians and Muslims, as-Sīsi is taking a moderate stand.

According to Nathan Brown, in 2015, as-Sīsi

> before an audience of religious leaders at al-Azhar... spoke of the need to "renew religious discourse." The president's words were strong... but also very general. It was clear they were aimed at religious thinking that Sisi held responsible from promoting extremism, terrorism, and violence. However, it was not clear if his target was the so-called Islamic State, the Muslim Brotherhood, radicals within al-Azhar's own ranks, more traditionally minded scholars seen as obscurantist and ineffectual rather than threatening, or a combination of these.[18]

In 2016, various institutions like the Ministry of Religious Affairs, the Office of the State Mufti, and the leadership of al-Azhar formulated responses to this speech. The latter welcomed the president's initiative but claimed to have already entered

[17] Aaron Rock-Singer, "Amr Khaled: From Daʿwa to Political and Religious Leadership," *The British Journal of Middle Eastern Studies* 37 (2010): 18.

[18] Nathan J. Brown, *Official Islam in the Arab World: The Contest for Religious Authority* (Washington, DC: Carnegie Endowment for International Peace, 2017), 19.

into a process of embracing a renewal of thinking, a process that should however be left to the experts within al-Azhar. Brown concludes: "That is, rather than taking the president's request as a challenge to its way of doing things, officials at al-Azhar, led by Sheikh Ahmad al-Tayyib himself, worked to appropriate the language in a manner that affirmed their own leadership."[19] Whether the renewal of Islamic thinking as-Sīsi called for will lead to a new appreciation of religious diversity, the recognition of human rights standards on religious freedom, and the full equality of rights of all citizens regardless of their religious affiliation, still remains to be seen.

On the basis of this historical overview, it is debatable whether full equality among people of different religious affiliation has been achieved in the Egyptian state and society, and whether equal rights for all citizens and full freedom of religion actually exist in the country. Since the majority of Egyptian citizens are Muslims, the question arises as to how the Christian churches there deal with this situation and how they try to work towards peaceful coexistence. We therefore now turn to initiatives by churches in the field of Christian-Muslim relations and dialogue.

1.3. Christian Churches in Egypt on the Question of Interreligious Dialogue

Just as in many other majority Muslim societies, there are relatively few interreligious dialogue initiatives in Egyptian society. That is not to say that Egyptians are not concerned about religious matters or the conflict between Muslims and Christians. Rather, the lack of dialogue initiatives in Egypt mostly arises because many Egyptians think that dialogue should be conducted by professional religious leaders. The tense atmosphere between Muslims and Christians may contribute to this shortage of initiatives. Despite the lack of dialogue initiatives in Egypt, the churches are making a big effort to achieve peace between Muslims and Christians. Before we discuss Christian dialogue initiatives, I should provide a summary of the religious statics of Egypt. It is very difficult to estimate the number of Christians in Egypt. No one really knows how many there are; estimates vary according to the sources. Muslims obviously constitute the majority. Egypt's population stands at around 104 million today, of which Muslims are said to account for between 85 percent and 90 percent, while Coptic Christians are believed to account for between 10 percent and 15 percent. This would mean that there are approximately 10 million Christians in Egypt.[20]

In the Middle East and North Africa, Egyptian Christians constitute the largest minority group. About 90 percent of these Christians belong to the Coptic Orthodox Church, followed by smaller communities of Protestants, Roman Catholics,

[19] Brown, *Official Islam*, 20.

[20] "Egypt's Sisi meets world Evangelical churches delegation in Cairo," Ahram Online (Sunday, November 19, 2017), http://english.ahram.org.eg/News/281789.aspx (accessed July 18, 2018).

independents, and others. Some Christians in Egypt have estimated their own number to be about 20 million. Others put the figure at about 16 million. Protestant churches claim to have a membership of about 2 million, and the Coptic Catholic Church is estimated to have half a million members in Egypt. These figures might be overestimated; Muslim sources regularly calculate the percentage of Christians to be far lower. Such estimations are ultimately a political matter, since the estimated percentages are generally instrumentalized either to support Christian aspirations to greater political influence or Muslim attempts to marginalize the Christian minority.

1.3.1. The Coptic Orthodox Church

For its size, the Coptic Orthodox Church has launched very few dialogue initiatives. Over the course of the 20th century, we can point to only a handful of attempts. For example, in 1985, a group of youth from the Coptic Orthodox Church decided to found the Cultural Development Group (CDG). This group in 1994 gave rise to the Coptic Center for Social Studies (CCSS). Later on, a course on cultural development was started, its primary focus being on Muslim-Christian relations. Two of its main aims were to build "bridges of dialogue" to the society and to encourage youth to participate in civil society more effectively. In its lectures, the CDG sometimes invited liberal Muslims as speakers, people who respect Christians and do not consider them *dhimmi* or call them a minority.

One important leader of the CDG named Samir Morqus viewed this attempt to establish better and closer ties as problematic because its proponents addressed only Christian audiences. How can dialogue come about or succeed when one main element, namely the Muslim party, is always absent? The initiative has also been afflicted by other problems that have been addressed by at least one prominent CCSS leader – problems like bureaucracy and conservatism.[21] It appears therefore that the initiative is more of a monologue than a dialogue, and that it takes place mainly behind closed doors and in theory, whereas almost nothing is practiced in reality.

There have also been other attempts to initiate better relations between the Coptic Orthodox Church and al-Azhar, such as *joint celebrations* when the fast is broken after Ramadan, or on Easter and Christmas. Such joint celebrations were launched as early as the 1919 revolution against British rule in Egypt and Sudan.[22] Now these meetings may indeed be positive, but they are restricted to the upper echelons and generally serve to maintain only surface-level, official relations. While they give "a nice face" to the interaction between the groups, they have little real impact on mutual understanding and do not lead to substantive discussions of theological differences.

Other meetings are sometimes held between the Coptic Orthodox Church, al-Azhar, and régime representatives. These meetings are held especially *after violent*

---

[21] Abū-Nimer, *Interfaith Dialogue*, 141-178.

[22] Henrik Lindberg Hansen, *Christian-Muslim Relations in Egypt: Politics, Society and Interfaith Encounters* (London: I.B. Tauris, 2015), 165-166.

incidents to calm down the public and to sustain *national unity*. These meetings are always publicized in the media and highlighted in public spaces to minimize the seriousness of the incident in question. Most of the time, they offer the same static analysis, blaming the incidents on enemies from abroad who seek to divide the nation.

One of the most important institutions for the Coptic Orthodox Church in this regard, on which it depends in terms of its social role, is the *Bishopric of Public, Ecumenical and Social Services*, established in 1962 to serve poor and disadvantaged communities. The bishopric runs a monthly assistance program for poor families, a program of assistance helping students get an education, and a program of assistance for young girls getting married. It also tries to help with unemployment and by financing small projects in villages.

In his official media statements, Pope Tawadros always underscores the long history of peaceful social coexistence between Muslims and Christians in Egypt. As an example of cooperation between Christians and Muslims, he sometimes mentions *Family House* (also known as *House of the Egyptian Family*), a project established by both the Coptic Orthodox Church and al-Azhar which is responsible for a number of national programs. Tawadros stresses that efforts must be stepped up to end the violence perpetrated by extremist Muslim groups.

1.3.2. The Protestant Church in Egypt (Nile Synod)

The Protestant Churches in Egypt (PCE) are made up of sixteen officially recognized Protestant denominations, the biggest one being the Evangelical Presbyterian Church in Egypt, also called the Synod of the Nile.[23] The Evangelical Presbyterian Church in Egypt was founded in the year 1854. From its beginnings, the church has been involved in local communities through social, educational, and medical programs. This church too has launched several projects promoting Christian-Muslim dialogue.[24] In 2014, the Evangelical Presbyterian Church's *Council of Ecumenical Relations and Dialogue* started a project involving a series of conferences and meetings between Muslim and Christian leaders. Their vision is to bring people together to talk, highlighting individual aspects of some public issues and creating opportunities to learn from and about each other. The Evangelical Presbyterian Council began hosting seminars to train leaders who are involved in dialogues in several areas in Egypt. The idea is for them to develop the needed skills to engage in positive and effective communication. Additionally, the Council organizes Christian-Muslim dialogue conferences to develop mutual understanding, respect, and fruitful interaction. They also promote ecumenical dialogue conferences between Orthodox, Catholic, and Evangelical (Protestant) churches.

[23] See Makari, *Conflict and Cooperation*.

[24] World Council of Churches, "Evangelical Presbyterian Church of Egypt Synod of the Nile," https://www.oikoumene.org/en/member-churches/evangelical-presbyterian-church-of-egypt-synod-of-the-nile (accessed July 18, 2018).

When describing the efforts of Egyptian Protestant Churches in the field of dialogue, mention should be made of the *Coptic Evangelical Organization for Social Services*, abbreviated CEOSS. It started as a literacy project in 1950 and is now one of the leading development bodies in Egypt.[25] It serves urban poor and rural communities in the areas of economics, agriculture, the environment, healthcare, and education. CEOSS encourages Muslims and Christians in Egypt to work together towards common goals. After about seventy years of experience, it has become a leader in the development of Egypt. CEOSS in the 1980s expanded its vision to develop cultural projects promoting dialogue, pluralism, and democracy. In 1992, it started a forum focusing on issues directly connected to cultural development: building tolerance, acceptance of others, and peaceful coexistence. This forum was established to support a culture of dialogue by fostering an atmosphere of mutual respect and acceptance of diversity. It aims to support social integration in order to help build a pluralistic society by targeting multiple categories of people such as intellectuals, opinion-makers, religious leaders, media professionals, and academics.

1.3.3. The Roman Catholic Church

The Roman Catholic Church has been present in Egypt for the last 800 years or so. Today, the Roman Catholic Church there comprises of about 30,000 members (led by the Apostolic Vicariate of Alexandria). In addition, a number of churches in Egypt are in fellowship with the Roman Catholic Church. The biggest of these united churches is the Coptic Catholic Church, comprising 250,000 members. A few observations about the question of interfaith relations may suffice for the purpose of this study. The Roman Catholic Church and churches in fellowship with the Roman Catholic Church are active in Egyptian society by way of a considerable number of social service projects and institutes, aiming to help and improve the lives of Egyptian people in general. According to Hansen, the Roman Catholic Church in Egypt has engaged in few dialogue efforts. Since the Roman Catholic Church has many different orders and organizations in addition to its church structure proper, it is not easy to provide an overview of its activities. As it is, dialogue efforts by the Roman Catholic Church are mostly initiatives by individuals. Representatives of the Roman Catholic Church are involved in the *Egyptian Committee for Justice and Peace* (ECJP). The aim is to engage in serious discussions about the real problems of society. The schools run by the Roman Catholic Church also adopted a kind of project concerned with interfaith dialogue. They organize meetings and summer camps for the students and teachers of their schools and invite both Muslim and Christian lecturers to take part.

Hansen lists the following kinds of dialogue in which the Roman Catholic Church is involved: firstly, dialogues promoted by different organizations and schools belonging to the Roman Catholic Church; secondly, academic dialogues undertaken mostly by Catholic monks; thirdly, dialogues promoting harmonious

[25] Makari, *Conflict & Cooperation*, 151-160.

coexistence in poor neighborhoods; and, fourthly, official dialogues between the Vatican in Rome and al-Azhar University.[26]

It is evident that the Roman Catholic Church is very active in the field of social services in Egyptian society. By way of active service, the Roman Catholic Church communicates with people from all walks of society in everyday life, be they Muslims or Christians; this amounts to a kind of dialogical activity on the social level. I would like briefly to mention examples of such social services organizations working with Muslims and Christians alike. *Sanabel* is a social association founded by Father Victor Juergi in 1950 to motivate the Christians of Egypt to contribute to the development of their country. Sanabel serves a part of Cairo known as the "gardens of the dome." It provides and runs medical services, nurseries, workshops, centers of maternity, childhood services, and social clubs.

Then there is the *Egyptian Committee for Justice and Peace*, a Christian organization founded in 1969. It aims to awaken the social conscience and to encourage everyone to work for the establishment of justice and peace in the world.

Another example is the *Caritas-Egypt Association*, a Christian association for social development affiliated to *Caritas International*, which has 162 branches spread throughout the world, sixteen of which are in Arab countries. In addition, we should mention in this regard the *Catholic Relief Foundation* and the *Saint Mansur Association*.[27]

1.3.4. The Anglican Church

The Anglican Church in Egypt is quite small in terms of the number of its members as compared to other Egyptian churches. It has about 20,000 members and consists of Egyptians, other Africans, and Western expatriates living in Egypt. The Anglican Church leadership actively promotes dialogue initiatives in order to improve its relationships with Muslims. There are three levels of dialogue in the Anglican Church. Firstly, the official dialogue with al-Azhar; secondly, initiatives on the grassroots level, including school projects; and, thirdly, the attempt to integrate elements of interreligious dialogue in its development initiatives. After September 11, 2001, an interfaith dialogue committee was jointly founded by al-Azhar al-Sharif and the Anglican Communion. This initiative brought together Egyptian religious leaders from both sides to work together for peace and dialogue and towards a greater understanding between Muslims and Christians. According to the website of the *Anglican Diocese of Egypt*, its interfaith dialogue initiatives include the following:

> A scholarly exchange between a theological college in Cambridge and al-Azhar University – The publication of books that clarify misconceptions involving Christianity and Islam – An interfaith conference for religious leaders from Sub-Saharan and North Africa – A

---

[26] Hansen, *Christian-Muslim Relations*, 184.

[27] Mutaffa Rahuma, "The Church in the Service of Society: Monthly Aid to Poor Families" (January 1, 2017), Al-Watan Newspaper, https://www.elwatannews.com/news/details/1735613 (accessed November 7, 2019).

program in Christian and Muslim schools called "Planting a Tree of Hope" – The joint visit of the Grand Mufti and Bishop Mouneer to Liverpool Hope University – A cooperative Fighting Blindness campaign headed by Harpur Memorial Hospital and Islamic charity Misr el-Kheir – The Arkan Centre, at St. Mark's Pro-Cathedral in downtown Alexandria, started in April 2011 to provide a place for Egyptian youth, both Christian and Muslim, to gather and to create art. – The "Imam-Priest Exchange," an interfaith initiative started in 2013 which brings together Muslim and Christian religious leaders in Egypt. – The annual Caravan Festival of the Arts, hosted at St John's Church in Maadi, aims to using the arts as a bridge for intercultural and inter-religious dialogue, and All Saints' Cathedral in Zamalek has also hosted interfaith art exhibitions.[28]

Once again, it is clear that dialogues are being promoted on different levels of society and in the form of various approaches.

1.3.5. Conclusion

The overview has shown that Christians comprise approximately 10 percent of the total population of Egypt and are spread across a number of different church bodies. Christian churches in Egypt are involved in interreligious relations via a variety of individual and institutional initiatives and social services. Their overall aim is to maintain good relations with representatives of the state as well as with important institutions of the Muslim side.

We will now proceed by reviewing a number of books in order to gain a closer look at the profiles of different dialogue initiatives.

1.4. Christian-Muslim Relations in Egypt – A Literature Review

In recent years, several valuable books and articles have been published on Christian churches in Egypt, especially on the Coptic Orthodox Church and on relations between Muslims and Christians. In this section, we will present a selection of these books, paying special attention to the following: *Christians versus Muslims in Egypt* (2003) by Sonia S. Hasan, *Conflict and Cooperation* (2007) by Peter E. Makari, and *Christian-Muslim Relations in Egypt* (2015) by Henrik Lindberg Hansen.

[28] Anglican Diocese of Egypt, http://dioceseofegypt.org/explore/ministries/other-ministries/interfaith-dialogue/ (accessed July 18, 2018).

1.4.1. Dialogue and Struggle – Sonia S. Hasan

In her book *Christians versus Muslims in Modern Egypt: The Century-Long Struggle for Coptic Equality*, published in 2003, the author Sonia S. Hasan provides an overview of the history of the *Coptic Orthodox Church.* The author devotes special attention to the revival which has taken place in the church since the beginning of the 20th century.[29] She shows how over the course of the century, the Coptic Orthodox Church became an increasingly integrated, organized, and hierarchized entity, while at the same time new forms of congregational life appeared that contributed significantly to the revival of church attendance, pilgrimages, youth work, social work, Coptic media, and the like. Hasan observes these changes against the backdrop of intensified tensions between the different religious camps. She concludes that full equality has not yet become a reality in the Egyptian society and state.

1.4.2. Dialogue and Levels of Cooperation – Peter E. Makari

In his book *Conflict and Cooperation: Christian-Muslim Relations in Contemporary Egypt,* released in 2007, the author Peter E. Makari distinguishes four segments or levels of society which are especially important in terms of interreligious relations.[30] He argues that the current situation can be understood best as the *interplay* between these segments, namely: firstly, governmental and legal policies; secondly, what he calls official religion, that is on the Muslim side al-Azhar University, the *Dar al-Ifta'* (the Islamic Office of Religious Pronouncements), and the state mufti, and on the Christian side the pope of the Coptic Orthodox Church and the president of the Protestant Churches of Egypt as the two largest church bodies in the country; thirdly, political parties; and, fourthly, nongovernmental organizations.

In each of these segments, questions of interreligious relations play a certain role. The author aims to demonstrate that "*in the midst of tension and actual conflict, numerous examples of cooperation can be found that not only are not anomalous but have served an important purpose.* ... The kinds of cooperation cited are not unique in times of heightened conflict."[31] Since the effects of dialogue initiatives are difficult to grasp on the grassroots level, Makari focuses on the level of official relations. He argues that religious identity, as important as it is, nevertheless remains only one aspect of people's identity, and that other aspects therefore also have to be considered.[32] The study focuses primarily on the examination of group interaction, as well as public rhetoric and activity. Makari concludes:

> Pluralistic societies in Egypt and the Arab world do not need to struggle to enjoy their full fruits; religious diversity can contribute to vi-

[29] Sonia S. Hasan, *Christians versus Muslims in Modern Egypt: The Century-Long Struggle for Coptic Equality* (Oxford: Oxford University Press, 2003).

[30] Makari, *Conflict & Cooperation.*

[31] Makari, *Conflict & Cooperation*, 190.

[32] Makari, *Conflict & Cooperation*, 197.

> brant civil society and indeed to peace making and in fact is doing so. In the clash of ideologies – conservative and exclusivist versus moderate and tolerant – seeking and modeling cross-communal co-operation among those who dream of more perfect social harmony can be important keys to reclaiming the discourse and the public debate.[33]

Whereas Peter E. Makari is concerned with the reality of interreligious activities between different actors in different segments of the society, Hendrik Lindberg Hansen focuses more on the underlying power relations as a key element to understand different kinds of interreligious dialogue.

1.4.3. Dialogue and Clientelism – Hendrik Lindberg Hansen

In his book *Christian-Muslim Relations in Egypt*, the author Hendrik Lindberg Hansen develops the argument that the meaning of *dialogue* in Egypt can be properly understood only if one considers the specific historical background as well as the political and social contexts. In Egyptian society, patron-client systems are very common. The régime tries to maintain its power by entertaining relations with different groups as a patron over against clients. The problem is that such patron-client relations undermine democratic structures and procedures. Only people who qualify as clients in some way may expect help from the government. The principle that the government should provide water, food, healthcare, education, and so forth for every citizen, regardless of who he or she is, is abandoned. This causes a lot of uncertainty for the majority of the population.

In this context, religious groups – Muslim organizations like the Muslim Brotherhood, or Christian churches like the Coptic Orthodox Church – are engaged in building networks to provide aid *for their members* at points where governmental structures fail, such as medical care, education, providing job opportunities, and the like. These religious networks occasionally compete with each other for resources. Without considering these circumstances, Hansen claims, it is not possible to understand the phenomenon of "dialogue" in Egyptian society. Hansen states:

> This system of clientelism is essential to understanding dialogue, as religion is an important factor in differentiating society into different groupings. Consequently, dialogue can work to both bridge and contest these gaps [for instance between rulers and ruled, city and rural areas, Muslims and Christians – FA] in society. In Egypt, the different types of dialogue are the language and tools by which some of the different groupings of society communicate. Dialogue then is not just discussion about religious issues. The system of patronage was the reason why some people saw the only valid aim of dialogue as uniting against the injustice in society; others saw dialogue as a

[33] Makari, *Conflict & Cooperation*, 208.

> means to further strengthen the ties between the religious institutions representing different parts of the society.[34]

Hansen differentiates in his typology between three approaches to dialogue: firstly, boxing match dialogue, secondly, official dialogue, and, thirdly, social dialogue.[35] The boxing match dialogue and official dialogue approaches share the assumption that different religious traditions are incompatible, since they have different ultimate truth claims. The boxing match dialogue is aimed at convincing the other of one's own truth, so that after debating the issues, one participant of the dialogue will be convinced of the truth of the other and therefore convert. Dialogue is therefore understood as a tool for and an invitation to conversion. To be specific, in this approach, dialogue aims at conversion. Now whereas boxing match dialogue is always concerned with religious matters, official dialogue explicitly avoids them. This applies to religious matters in general and to religious truth claims in particular. Whereas boxing match dialogue is something that happens once in a while in everyday life between ordinary people, official dialogue takes place particularly between high representatives of different religious traditions like the sheikh of al-Azhar or the pope of the Coptic Orthodox Church. On a lower level, similar official dialogues take place between highly respected persons from various local communities. Official dialogues are aimed at maintaining peaceful relations, and especially during those times when incidents like attacks on churches or riots occur.

In recent years, attacks on Christians or Christian churches have been ignored by the state-dominated press. The régime often tries to maintain the image of Egypt as a peaceful country where no real problems between the different religions exist. The motive behind this is apparently the attempt to avoid negative effects on the tourism industry or on foreign investments in Egypt. Hansen differentiates between *everyday incidents* like discrimination of religious minorities in everyday life, and *grand events*.[36] Media reports about *grand events* (like bombings) may increase the feeling of minorities that they are being discriminated against. Official dialogues often function as tools to calm down emotions by showing that high-ranking officials of different religions are willing to cooperate. As Hansen puts it:

> These discourses... are fundamental in connecting the actual incidents with the efforts of dialogue, as they potentially encourage reluctance to admit problems and thereby help maintain the status quo, or alternatively as they have the potential to break down negative definitions of religious identity against the religious other by superimposing a feeling of national unity.[37]

[34] Hansen, *Christian-Muslim Relations*, 85.

[35] Hansen, *Christian-Muslim Relations*, 4, 154-215.

[36] Hansen, *Christian-Muslim Relations*, 111.

[37] Hansen, *Christian-Muslim Relations*, 112.

The third approach to dialogue, social dialogue, also avoids religious matters. It is aimed at cooperation mainly on the grassroots level. According to Hansen, dialogue always has to do with power. Whereas French philosopher Michel Foucault defines power primarily as non-subjective or impersonal force, Hansen, appealing to John C. Turner, understands power in dialogue as a *subject-oriented force* operating on three levels: as convincing power, as authoritative power, and as coercing power.[38] Hansen writes:

> This understanding of power is, however, not only relevant to the understanding of Egyptian society but also to the understanding of what dialogue is – in so far as dialogue is seen as the negotiation of relations between societal groups. It provides a means of determining which people are essential to different types of dialogue and it can demonstrate how people are influenced by dialogue.[39]

Hansen shows that the system of clientelism plays an important role not only for al-Azhar University, but also for the Coptic Orthodox Church. This system is likely to affirm the differences between Muslims and Christians, since it has to do with resources and recognition and is a means to further one's influence in the wider society.

Now whereas Hansen develops an understanding of dialogue which is able to consider different kinds of power relations and to view dialogue as a means to deal with differences within these multiple kinds of relatedness, Hussein Hamdan solely focuses on the few dialogue initiatives undertaken by representatives of al-Azhar University.

1.4.4. Attempts by Al-Azhar University to Engage in Dialogue – Hussein Hamdan

In his work *Der christlich-islamische Dialog der Azhar-Universität*, the author Hussein Hamdan traces the topic of dialogue back to the 1930s, when two al-Azhar scholars took part in two conferences held in Europe: one in London (1936) and the other in Paris (1939). The author admits that up until now, dialogue events have been initiated almost entirely by Christian activists, whereas Azhari scholars have only reacted to invitations.[40] The source material Hamdan uses is the journal *Majallat al-Azhar*. Even at the beginning of the 21st century, scholars were still referring to the contributions made by the two Azhari scholars in the 1930s.[41] Now while talks about refuting atheism and communism are cited, dialogues about creeds and faith find hardly any mention.[42]

---

[38] Hansen, *Christian-Muslim Relations*, 169.

[39] Hansen, *Christian-Muslim Relations*, 170.

[40] Hussein Hamdan, (Der christlich-islamische Dialog der Azhar-Universität. Freiburg: Herder, 2014), 104 ff.

[41] Hamdan, *Dialog*, 121ff.

[42] Hamdan, *Dialog*, 132, 148ff.

The author summarizes the intentions of al-Azhar over the course of almost a century as the desire to find a basis for practical cooperation in the attempt to promote peace and tolerance. Hamdan cites *Mahmud Shaltut* as an important voice representing the moderate stream. He explains that from 1978 to 1985, the Azhari agenda was: *No dialogue about creeds* (*lā ḥiwār fī al-'aqā'id* in Arabic)!

Hamdan's findings may be summarized as follows: Considering that al-Azhar University as an organization comprises more than 7 percent of the entire Egyptian educational sector, it is safe to state that its dialogue initiatives have been and continue to be negligible at best.

1.4.5. Interfaith Activities under Suspicion – Muḥammad Abū-Nimer

In his 2007 book *Unity in Diversity: Interfaith Dialogue in the Middle East*, the author Muḥammad Abū-Nimer finds that there is widespread suspicion in Egyptian society about interfaith activities, since they are seen to be imposed by agents from the West.[43] As far as the present situation is concerned, Abū-Nimer states that there are still obstacles to interfaith dialogue such as "the overpoliticization of dialogue efforts, the deficiency of grassroots initiatives, the suspicion surrounding dialogue efforts, and the lack of a clear vision for dialogue."[44] Since the question of national unity is of utmost importance, interfaith initiatives by armed groups may be regarded as affirming the rifts in society in that they focus not on common ground, but on the differences between religious camps. Many Egyptians regard interfaith activities as financed and directed by NGO's or governments from Western countries and thus as thinly-disguised attempts to interfere in Egyptian affairs. Social contacts between Christians and Muslims are widely regarded as a purely ethical affair, for instance when adherents of the different faiths congratulate each other during religious feast seasons. Besides, social life is often seen as an autonomous domain, since both mosques and churches provide a wide range of social services and activities for leisure time. Meanwhile, the government all too often fails to provide even basic medical, educational, or social services.

An overview of Abū-Nimer clearly shows that interreligious dialogue in the typical Western understanding is almost absent in Egypt. He calls for local, indigenized "Egyptian" initiatives on the grassroots level which are conceived of, organized, and conducted by Egyptians for Egyptians. With regard to the past, Abū-Nimer concludes:

> The rise of Islamism in the 1970s made the core question of interfaith relations in Egypt one of citizenship. Much effort, work, writing, and discussions situated the Coptic question in this framework. This conceptualization of the problem was good for the 1970s, but today, it risks adding to the undesired overpoliticization of dialogue. Social manifestations of sectarian conflict, which are currently considered

[43] Abū-Nimer, *Interfaith Dialogue*, 141-169.

[44] Abū-Nimer, *Interfaith Dialogue*, 165.

> minor or incidental, should be taken more seriously. The core question now is social relations; it is about the highly competitive social environment between Muslims and Christians. A political approach is necessary and important only if it is supported by social and cultural approaches as well.[45]

Abū-Nimer argues that a variety of different initiatives is needed. Whereas Copts have acquired some knowledge of Islam, according to Abū-Nimer,

> Muslim's knowledge about Christianity in general and Coptic Christianity in particular is too scant. As Coptic initiatives to spread knowledge about Christianity have been perceived suspiciously as missionary work to convert Muslims, efforts to pursue and spread such knowledge must be initiated by Muslims. Popular writings, articles, booklets, curricula, and different audiovisual materials need to be created and put at the Muslim's disposal so that they can choose to learn more about their neighbor's history and legacy. Materials about Muslims and their heritage should also be made available to Copts, as such knowledge must be mutual.[46]

Abū-Nimer's demands bring us to the core concern of this study, namely how al-Azhar University scholars approach the task of comparing different religions and teaching about the religion of the Other, in this case: the Christian religion. This question will be addressed in the main chapters of this study.

1.4.6. Conclusion

The review of recent books on Christian-Muslim relations in Egypt has shown that there is a broad variety of initiatives on the part of different Christian churches aimed at promoting social relations between people of different religious backgrounds. But the churches are only one player in this field, albeit a very significant one. Non-governmental organizations also engage in this field, focusing particularly on social issues and not on political or theological matters. Overall, it would be fair to say that in the context of Egypt, dialogue on this level is rarely understood as theological debate. Very often, actors prefer to pass over theological matters in order to avoid topics that could cause tensions between people. It is evident that not only are a variety of actors engaged in social affairs and interfaith matters, but it is also necessary to distinguish between different levels at which dialogues are held, such as the level of local neighborhoods, the level of state policies, and the level of public opinion and the media. Egyptian society has undergone a lot of changes especially concerning the public space and media. This is a field of study of its own and is not to be addressed here.

---

[45] Abū-Nimer, *Interfaith Dialogue*, 167.

[46] Abū-Nimer, *Interfaith Dialogue*, 168.

An important point is the fact that in present-day Egyptian society, the patron-client system continues to play a major role in social and political matters. "Dialogue" therefore has to be regarded in the framework of power relations. In other words: There is no free space, there is no way of describing dialogical activities without considering that *words* are only one aspect of the phenomenon; many challenges and problems which have a bearing on the respective issue frequently *go unmentioned*. We have to follow Hansen in recognizing that on the social level, people often avoid matters of faith and creed, and the same goes for the political level. Theological matters do however play a role in interfaith talks in everyday life whenever the so-called "boxing match dialogue" (Hansen) can be observed.

This leads us to an important observation: Egyptians regard each other not only as citizens of one and the same nation but also as adherents of different creeds and therefore of different camps. The theological framework of the Muslim worldview constitutes one universe of meaning, while the theological framework of the Christian worldview constitutes another. Even though these worldviews are not the only factor which influences the behavior and actions of people, these worldviews are certainly important to consider.

1.5. Purpose Statement, Sources, and Methodological Approach

Consequently, it is necessary and helpful to raise the following questions: Who are the main actors shaping a particular understanding of "Islam" and "Christianity" in Egyptian society? What are the major educational institutions in this field? How do scholars from these institutions think about the other religion – or more specifically, what do Muslim scholars think about other religions in general and about Christianity in particular? How do they interpret their own religious heritage and the holy scriptures of the other religion? What methodological approaches do they use in order to understand the other religion? Are they able to treat the other religion with respect? And what does that mean? In which way do theological interpretations of the *religious Other* promote peaceful and respectful relations between people of different faiths?

With regard to Egypt, al-Azhar University is by far the most important actor as far as the Muslim side is concerned. For that reason, the purpose of this study is to analyze works of Muslim scholars at al-Azhar University working in the field of the comparison of religions (*muqāranat al-adyān* in Arabic). How do they approach other religions methodologically? What is the theological outcome of the comparison? Are the attempts to compare different religions solely grounded in an Islamic understanding of different topics, or do these scholars try to understand other religions within the respective frameworks of those religions – that is, do they understand Christian teachings within the framework of the Christian scriptures, traditions, teachings, and doctrines? Do these comparisons open up spaces for mutual understanding and recognition?

In raising questions like these, it is important to reflect on the sources that are selected. Since there are so many scholars at al-Azhar University, it would simply be impossible to take them all into account. Due to spatial limitations, this study will limit itself to analyzing three important scholars. Since very few dialogue initiatives have been launched thus far, one might be tempted to choose the one or two authors who best fit the expectations of a Western audience – that is, to choose scholars who are exceptional in that they plead for a "dialogical" approach to religious studies. But to the best of my knowledge, almost no such scholars serve at al-Azhar University. It would seem to me to be far more relevant and of far greater importance to select scholars who represent mainstream thinking. The works of such scholars might not be described as *innovative*, but they would at least be *representative*. In my view, it is necessary to take into account the present realities of interfaith relations, not to invoke some "vision" of a future – as desirable as that may be – which does not currently exist. Consequently, this study is not about elitist discourses conducted on the international level between a select few individuals for the sake of publicity. Instead, it is about ordinary scholars who train large numbers of people who – after their studies – will serve in state institutions and other areas of society, where they will also have a certain amount of influence on interfaith relations at different levels of society.

This means that the very *selection* of scholars to be analyzed here is *in itself* already of methodological relevance. The selection parameters reflect my understanding of the importance of these ordinary scholars with regard to Muslim-Christian relations, since in some ways, these scholars train a significant number of people who later on will assume key positions in Egyptian society.

Methodologically, the selected works on the topic of the *comparison of religions* by Muslim scholars of al-Azhar University will be analyzed systematically with regard to the following questions: How do these works represent the faith or creed of the other (Christian) religion? What is their exegetical, doctrinal, and hermeneutical approach? What kind of methodology do they apply? What kind of Islamic sources do they use? Are they familiar with Christian theological traditions and sources? What language skills do they exhibit? What kind of interreligious dialogue – if any – do they promote? What is their understanding of the "comparison of religions"?

It is my conviction that the way in which different religions are compared has a significant impact on the way adherents of other religions are regarded. Even though the theological matrix is only one factor in a wide range of different forces determining human behavior and thinking, it is an important one. This study focuses on al-Azhar University as a very large player in the field of interreligious relations in Egypt, since its scholars play an important role, as do their teachings on the comparison of religions. Even though their influence on Egyptian society is hard to quantify, it is safe to assume that they have a considerable impact on it – certainly on the microlevel of everyday life, but perhaps also on the social and political levels of society, given that alumni of al-Azhar may well get to serve in posts in administration and politics where they would act as decision makers.

1.6. Outline

The study is comprised of three parts. Part 1, entitled *Interreligious Relations in Egypt: Al-Azhar and the Christian Churches*, serves to provide the necessary basic information on al-Azhar University as a Muslim institution of higher learning. Addressing the question of *Who speaks for Islam in Egypt? – The Role of al-Azhar*, this part begins with a historical sketch and information on the role of al-Azhar graduates, the influence of al-Azhar, and the brand of Islam for which al-Azhar claims to stand. With al-Azhar being an important political player in Egyptian society, some of its officials and their position on matters of interreligious dialogue are then considered, followed by a brief overview of some well-known al-Azhar scholars writing on the topic of the Christian faith from a Muslim perspective. These chapters provide information on the views of al-Azhar officials and scholars concerning the relations between Islam/Islamic teachings and Christianity/Christian doctrine. Taken together, Part 1 supplies the background against which works by three 20th century al-Azhar scholars will be analyzed.

In Part 2, *Islamic Al-Azhar Scholars on the Comparison of Religions*, the study will assess the work of Maḥmūd ʻAlī ʻAbdel Raḥmān Ḥimāiyah, Taha Rayyān, and Ahmad Shalabi. Part 2 then goes on to report and draw on interviews held with representative Christian and Muslim authorities on present-day Muslim-Christian relations in Egypt, followed by a summary of the various positions.

In Part 3, *Towards a Better Understanding*, the study evaluates the findings that were made. It then goes on to offer suggestions as to future cooperation between Muslims and Christians in the quest of coming to a more appropriate understanding of each other.

Part I.

Interreligious Relations in Egypt: Al-Azhar and the Churches

2. Who speaks for Islam in Egypt? – The Role of Al-Azhar

2.1. Al-Azhar Mosque and University: An Historical Introduction

In this chapter, I will present a brief review about al-Azhar's history. Al-Azhar Mosque is an Egyptian mosque in Islamic Cairo. The name "al-Azhar" may be translated as "the most splendid."[1] The term *Jāmi'* is derived from the Arabic root word *jama'a* (j-m-'), meaning "to come together." *Jāmi'* is generally used for large congregational mosques. On the orders of Caliph al-Mu'izz li-Din Allah of the Fatimid dynasty, the Fatimid general Gawhar al-Ṣiqillī, a former Greek slave from Sicily, constructed Cairo as the new capital city of Egypt in 969. This construction included a great mosque originally named according to the name of the capital city, but later named al-Azhar.

Under the rule of the Fatimids, al-Azhar was an important institution for promulgating the Shia-teachings of the rulers. The influence of al-Azhar declined under the reign of the Sunni Ayyubid dynasty, 1171-1249. From 1250-1517 (648-922 H.), Egypt was ruled by the Mamluk dynasty. During this time, the influence of al-Azhar as a Sunni school of learning grew constantly. The sultans and emirs who reigned after 1517 supported al-Azhar through endowments. After the end of the Muslim rule of Al-Andalus, the universities in that part of the world closed down. As a result, the number of students at al-Azhar increased significantly. Al-Azhar may rightly be called a university in the modern sense of the word from the 1950s on, when a new system of learning was introduced. In 2013, the university, now comprising seventy different faculties, was decentralized, with branches being created all across Egypt.

2.1.1. The Role of Al-Azhar in Society at Large

Al-Azhar is a famous institution in Egyptian society, but its role has changed significantly over the last 150 years. Some aspects deserve mention in this regard. Firstly, one has to take into account the growing influence of Islam in Egypt since the late 19th century. Nathan Brown maintains that Islam was not even mentioned in the 1882 constitution of Egypt, and that the constitution of 1923 contains only

[1] Heinz Halm, *Die Kalifen von Kairo: Die Fatimiden in Ägypten 973-1074* (Munich: Beck, 2003).

vague hints about the Islamic nature of politics.[2] During the era of al-Nāṣīr, Islam is also mentioned only briefly in the constitution, but under the rule of President as-Sādāt, the constitution was changed in 1971. Sharia was now said to be "a primary source of legislation." In the constitution of 1980, the position of Islam is strengthened once more, to the effect that sharia is now "the primary source of legislation."[3] But how is this phrase to be understood? Brown states:

> At its most ambitious, it seemed to incorporate the Islamic sharia into the constitutional order itself, requiring that ordinary legislation be drawn from, and be fully compliant with, the sharia. (This position became easier to argue after 1980, when the wording was amended to make *sharia* principles *the* rather than *a* primary source of legislation.) But far more modest readings of the provision were also possible – that it was merely a statement of fact or a vague directive to parliamentarians to consult the Islamic legal heritage for undefined 'principles' as part of the legislative process. And nowhere did the article make clear how it could be enforced or was even meant to be enforced.[4]

The constitution of 1971 does not deal with the position of the state mufti, the role of al-Azhar, the structure of law courts, religious endowments, and mosques. Brown interprets this fact as proof that the reference to Islam is rather symbolic in nature. The constitution is aimed at giving the state authorities power over religious matters:

> When the symbolic provisions of the Egyptian constitutional order are viewed in the context of the political structures that they enable, a single version of Islam emerges – one that is decreed, designed, organized, defined, regulated, inculcated, and policed by the state.[5]

Thereby the president exerts power not only over al-Azhar, but also over the ministry of religious endowments (*auqāf* in Arabic) and the *Dar al-Ifta'*. The president has the right to appoint the head of al-Azhar and the head of *Dar-al-Ifta'*. Furthermore the president appoints the minister of religious affairs and the prime minister. Both of them are responsible for the control of al-Azhar. Concerning courts of religious law, Brown states: "The version of religious law that the personal status courts apply is largely legislated by the parliament. Thus, the constitutional order induces Egyptian society to defer to state legislation in interpreting and applying religious teachings in the most intimate sphere."[6]

Since then the role of the president and the parliament in controlling Islamic affairs has been far-reaching. As Brown puts it:

---

[2] Brown, *Islam*.

[3] Brown, *Islam*, 236.

[4] Brown, *Islam*, 236-237.

[5] Brown, *Islam*, 238.

[6] Brown, *Islam*, 239.

> Thus, the constitution as it has been implemented has placed tremendous authority in the hands of the executive, legislative, and judicial branches to interpret and apply Islam. And it should be repeated as well that Article 19 required the state not merely to interpret and apply Islam but also to teach it to children – and therefore to develop a canonical version suitable for inculcation.[7]

All power rests in the hands of the president, but other actors play a role as well. This raises the question: Who has been speaking for Islam in Egypt since the 1970s? Besides the president, it has been the ministry of education, the ministry of religious endowments, the *Dar al-Ifta'*, and, last but not least, al-Azhar University. Even though there are a number of other universities in Egypt, the role of al-Azhar is still the most influential. Brown states:

> University faculties as institutional bodies do not challenge the role of al-Azhar as the state's premier Islamic and sometimes authoritative voice of Islam, but their existence makes possible an important source of expertise and supports a number of critical intellectuals able to provide expert advice and public commentary.[8]

2.1.2. The Role of Graduates of Al-Azhar – the Employment of 'Ulamā' in Egypt

Since Egypt has become a nation state, significant reforms have taken place. In the 1870s and 1880s, traditional sharia courts were replaced by a new court system. The government introduced mixed courts, where jurists from other countries were employed in addition to Egyptians. Secondly, national courts were founded, and, thirdly, religious courts. The latter remained a domain of the *'ulamā'*.[9] The *'ulamā'* may be defined as "the learned of Islam, those who possess the quality of *'ilm*, 'learning,' in its widest sense"[10] – they are therefore Islamic scholars in the broad sense. In 1956, sharia courts were abandoned. Skovgaard-Petersen states:

> From then onwards Azhar *'ulama* would be forced to compete with graduates of all other law faculties for employment in the courts, and the most important career ladder for top *'ulama* was gone. The state was now in more direct control of a unified legal system through the

[7] Brown, *Islam*, 239.

[8] Brown, *Islam*, 241.

[9] Jakob Skovgaard-Petersen, "Egypt's 'Ulama in the State, in Politics, and in the Islamist Vision," in Said Amir Arjomand and Nathan J. Brown, eds., *The Rule of Law, Islam, and Constitutional Politics in Egypt and Iran* (New York: State University of New York Press, 2013).

[10] Encyclopaedia Britannica, Britannica.com, s.v. *'ulamā'*, https://www.britannica.com/topic/ulama (accessed November 7, 2019).

> Ministry of Justice. The ministry itself has never been a significant employer of *'ulama*.[11]

This observation is important because it shows that graduates of al-Azhar fill important posts in the state apparatus. Even if the influence of scholars of al-Azhar cannot be measured, it seems obvious that there is at least some influence. Whatever scholars of al-Azhar teach concerning Christian-Muslim relations is likely to have some effect on the graduates now serving in the administration of the state.

It should also be mentioned that after the post of the state mufti was abandoned in 1895, it gained new importance in the 1970s again, since the government was struggling against political and radical Islam. Skovgaard-Petersen states:

> From the early 1990s the administration of the Mufti has grown significantly, and the present Mufti, Ali Gumaa, has set out on an ambitious plan to reform ifta and train muftis from abroad. An employee at the Ministry of Justice, the Mufti is a fairly reliable supporter of régime policies, and fully financed by the state.[12]

The ministry of religious endowments has also been gaining in influence. Today, it is responsible for the building and maintaining of mosques, the salaries of the staff of some mosques, and the official teaching concerning the Qur'an, as well as the

> institutes of *da'wa*, caravans of *da'wa* and teaching in the countryside, and special organizational tasks during hajj pilgrimage season, the holy month of Ramadan, Mulid al-Nabi (the birthday of the prophet), and other religious festivals and occasions. A special branch of the Ministry is the Supreme Council for Islamic Affairs which organizes international conferences and publications and sends teachers abroad.[13]

In the 1970s, the ministry of al-Azhar was founded. Today, the "second major employer of *'ulama* is the Ministry of al-Azhar."[14] This ministry administrates the national branch of al-Azhar, foreign students, and a significant part of the Egyptian school system that is under the aegis of al-Azhar and parallels the governmental schooling system. Currently about 7 percent of all students in Egypt are enrolled at al-Azhar schools which consist of primary schools (*kuttab* in Arabic) and secondary schools (*ma'had* in Arabic), with another 500,000 students enrolled at al-Azhar University and its branches. Al-Azhar appoints its own graduates at all levels of education.[15]

This institutional backing has to be taken into account when speaking about the influence of al-Azhar University in Egypt.

---

[11] Skovgaard-Petersen, *Egypt's 'Ulama*, 281.

[12] Skovgaard-Petersen, *Egypt's 'Ulama*, 281.

[13] Skovgaard-Petersen, *Egypt's 'Ulama*, 282.

[14] Skovgaard-Petersen, *Egypt's 'Ulama*, 282.

[15] Skovgaard-Petersen, *Egypt's 'Ulama*, 284.

2.1.3. The International Influence of Al-Azhar via Scholarships and the Media

The international influence of al-Azhar University is manifold. According to *Masooda Bano*, about 30,000 students from all over the world are enrolled at al-Azhar University. Al-Azhar itself provides scholarships for 4 percent of these students, which means that there are approximately 1,200 international scholarship holders at al-Azhar per year. This ensures the influence of al-Azhar by creating networks of personal relationships extending over many countries. The remaining 96 percent of scholarships are provided by foreign governments, foreign institutions, and private donors from foreign countries. This implies that there is an international need for educated personnel who would be labeled as adhering to a "moderate" understanding of Islam. Furthermore, the alumni themselves continually try to expand the network of relations, as has been done for hundreds of years. Most international students are enrolled in the three faculties of Islamic studies, where they generally acquire a Bachelor's Degree (BA) after four years of study and a Master's Degree (MA) after two additional years of education. A few students go on to obtain a Doctoral Degree (PhD) in Islamic studies. In the academic year 2012/13, the international students at al-Azhar hailed from 103 countries, with about 5,000 students coming from Arabic countries, 4,000 from African countries, 13,300 from Asia, and 2,900 students from European countries and especially from Russia. Approximately 900 students came from the Americas. A third of the students were female.[16]

In addition, al-Azhar also sends its lecturers to different countries around the world, and it also releases *fatwas*, publishes print media like *al-Azhar Magazine* and *Daut al-Azhar*, presents television broadcasts, and hosts internet pages. The *fatwas* released by al-Azhar are recognized in many countries of the world. In recent years, governmental representatives of Western countries tried to work together with al-Azhar to develop a curriculum for Muslim scholars in Western countries.[17] The political stance of al-Azhar is a subject of ongoing debate.[18]

2.1.4. The Brand of Islam Promoted by Al-Azhar: Al-Wasaṭiyya

Al-Azhar claims to determine its religious direction (*qibla* in Arabic) independently. This suggests that al-Azhar seeks to remain as independent as possible from both the Egyptian government and organizations like the Muslim Brother-

[16] Masooda Bano, "Protector of the 'al-Wasatiyya' Islam: Cairo's al-Azhar University," in Masooda Bano and Keiko Sakurai, eds., *Shaping Global Islamic Discourses: The Role of al-Azhar, al-Medina and al-Mustafa* (Edinburgh: Edinburgh University Press, 2015), 75-76.

[17] Bano, *Protector*, 73-90.

[18] Steven Barraclough, "Al-Azhar: Between the Government and the Islamists," *Middle East Journal* 52 (1998): 236-249; Meir Hatina, "Historical Legacy and the Challenge of Modernity in the Middle East: The Case of al-Azhar in Egypt," *The Muslim World* 93 (2003): 51-68.

hood. The government for its part is interested in maintaining good relations with al-Azhar because it depends on its backing in terms of religious legitimization. Therefore the government tries to avoid exercising too much influence on al-Azhar. It would seem that the Egyptian state and al-Azhar are in some ways mutually dependent.[19] For many years now, al-Azhar has been claiming to follow a moderate understanding of Islam called the "middle way" or *al-wasaṭiyya* in Arabic. According to Bano's research, which she conducted by way of interviews, though there are both students and professors at al-Azhar with *Salafīyyah* backgrounds, the university itself holds to a moderate or centrist understanding of Islam. What this comes down to is that multiple views and discourses are allowed at al-Azhar in a spirit of tolerance and debate, while in the curriculum of al-Azhar the teachings of all four key traditional Sunni schools of Islamic law are covered. At the same time, it is possible to do research on Sufism and Shia Islam as well, and even issues of religious plurality can be discussed.[20] According to Bano, al-Azhar serves as a *buffer zone* between radical Islam and political Islam, on the one hand, and state Islam, on the other. Prominent Salafi scholars at al-Azhar like Mohammad Hassan, Syed Ali Raza, or Safari Hajazi frequently speak on public television channels like *al-Rahman* or *al-Hafiz*.[21]

2.1.5. Rifts between Al-Azhar Officials and 'Ulamā' of Lower Rank

Makari points out that the *'ulamā'* of al-Azhar are very diverse. There are rifts within al-Azhar ranks, since some *'ulamā'* mainly support the government position, whereas other *'ulamā'* criticize it.[22] Zeghal differentiates between center and periphery at al-Azhar. He argues that

> within the political framework of the 1970s and the 1980s, al-Azhar as an institution tried to take part in the public debates raised by the emergence of radical Islam. Because the religious arena became more competitive, and because the Islamists challenged the legitimacy of al-Azhar, al-Azhar re-emerged as a political actor and started intervening in the public space. Its failure to make its voice heard in the mid-1970s entailed a growing political diversification within the body of the ulema. 'Peripheral ulema' emerged and distanced themselves from the official voice of al-Azhar through their practice of *da'wa* (the call to religion, especially by preaching) and introduced the different colors of Islamism into al-Azhar. Moreover, the emergence of violence on the Egyptian scene in the second half of the 1980s led most official ulema to reactivate their functions as

[19] Bano, *Protector*, 77-78.

[20] Bano, *Protector*, 80-81.

[21] Bano, *Protector*, 82-83.

[22] Makari, *Conflict & Cooperation*, 92-96.

> political brokers. Therefore, al-Azhar lost the monolithic and monopolistic nature Nasser had given it and became a plural and diversified body that is now itself in competition with other religious entrepreneurs. The idea of a monopoly of al-Azhar on religious interpretation is today questioned even among the most official ulema of al-Azhar, who recognize pluralism in religious thought.[23]

Among well-known al-Azhar scholars, a number disagree with the official position of al-Azhar leadership. Makari notes:

> Among those Azharis who have publicly expressed opinions in contradiction with the official government policy are *sheikh al-Azhar* 'Abd al- Halim Mahmud, who in the 1970s called for the transformation of the legal system at a time when Sadat was not supportive of the idea; Shaykhs Kishk, Mahallawi, and Salah Abu Isma'il, who did not participate in a government campaign to engage in dialogue at the local level with Islamist youth; Sheikh 'Atiyya Saqr, who demanded the implementation by Parliament of the *sharia* in 1984; and, perhaps most notably, Sheikh 'Umar 'Abd ar-Rahman, who has been accused and sentenced for inspiring *al-jama'a al-islamiyya.* ... These persons are all Azharis, and to varying degrees represent the institution's official stances. ... Even if they have moved to the periphery, their public association with al-Azhar has not been broken. Al-Azhar, therefore, can be said to carry the official government line while some of its "representatives" are in disagreement with the government or even closely affiliated with a very extreme brand of Islam. Great diversity thus exists.[24]

These examples clearly show that one cannot speak of "the" one single theological stance of al-Azhar. When in the 1990s the influence of television, satellite television, and the internet steadily grew, al-Azhar as an institution gradually took on the role of censorship by means of its *Academy of Islamic Research.* The academy was asked by the Egyptian government to approve such things as editions of the Qur'an and collections of the Ḥadīth, and the government then followed the academy's opinions. In this way, al-Azhar took on the role of legitimizing government policy. Skovgaard-Petersen explains: "The regime has had to accept the interference of al-Azhar in cultural life as a price to be paid for its loyalty, or even perhaps to strengthen the religious authority of the top *'ulama* it was relying on, as they were increasingly criticized for being government stooges."[25] Being regarded as puppets of the régime meant that a lot of high-ranking scholars of al-Azhar lost their credibility in the eyes of Islamists and *'ulamā'* of lower ranks. In the 1990s, a dormant organization called *Front of the Azhar Scholars* was revived in order to

[23] Malika Zeghal, "Religion and Politics in Egypt: The Ulema of al-Azhar, Radical Islam, and the State (1952-94)," *International Journal of Middle East Studies* 31 (1999): 372.
[24] Makari, *Conflict & Cooperation*, 94.
[25] Skovgaard-Petersen, *Egypt's Ulama*, 284.

criticize al-Azhar officials seen as being too close to the government. In 1999, the sheikh of al-Azhar decided to have this organization closed down. The government followed suit and closed it down in the same year. This shows the great importance of the sheikh of al-Azhar and the power he has. Skovgaard-Petersen: "At al-Azhar itself, the Shaykh al-Azhar controls the funds, the hiring, and the promotions and has thus, much like the general strategy of the regime, been able to pursue a policy of rewarding loyalists, coopting critics, and punishing opponents."[26]

2.1.6. Conclusion

One may conclude that al-Azhar apparently does not speak with one voice. Then again, the stance of al-Azhar officials like the Grand Sheikh of al-Azhar are of great importance for Egyptian society. Therefore we will now proceed by conducting a brief survey of recent utterances by al-Azhar officials on interreligious matters.

2.2. Al-Azhar officials on interreligious relations

2.2.1. Jād al-Ḥaqq 'Alī Jād al-Ḥaqq (Grand Sheikh 1982-1996)

In 1984, the Grand Sheikh of al-Azhar, Jād al-Ḥaqq 'Alī Jād al-Ḥaqq explicitly rejected a dialogue on religious belief, whereas he supported Muslim participation in interreligious conferences. His reasoning was that participating in, say, conferences held by European universities, government, or other organizations would give al-Azhar scholars the opportunity to represent Islam and Islamic teaching properly, thereby calling the audience to Islam.

2.2.2. Muḥammad Sayyid Ṭanṭāwī (Grand Sheikh 1996-2010)

According to Hussein Hamdan, things changed under the auspices of the new Grand Sheikh of al-Azhar, Muḥammad Sayyid Ṭanṭāwī. To sum up:[27] After a long period of criticism over against the Vatican, change came about through the engagement of Cardinal König who convinced Grand Sheikh Jād al-Ḥaqq in 1994 to establish official relations of some kind between the Vatican and al-Azhar.[28] The Grand Sheikh appointed Maḥmūd Zaqzūq to represent al-Azhar in the preliminary discussions.

When Jād al-Ḥaqq died, his successor Muḥammad Sayyid Ṭanṭāwī continued the discussions with the Vatican and was in favor of a dialogue being launched. In 1998, the *Agreement between the Pontifical Council for Interreligious Dialogue (Vatican City) and the Permanent Committee of al-Azhar for Dialogue with the Monotheistic Religions (Cairo) for the Creation of a Joint Committee for Dialogue*

[26] Skovgaard-Petersen, *Egypt's Ulama*, 285.

[27] Hamdan, *Dialog*, 222-300.

[28] Hamdan, *Dialog*, 249.

was signed by Cardinal Franzis Arinze and Sheikh Fauzī az-Zafzāf.[29] In this way, a dialogue platform between al-Azhar and the Vatican was created, known as the *Commission for the Dialogue of the Heavenly Religions*. Relations with the archbishop of Canterbury were also intensified.[30] As far as the *Commission* is concerned, it was comprised of six representatives from the Vatican and al-Azhar. Its purpose was to identify common ground, address common values, work for justice and peace, and to deal with any incidents that may arise. One gathering was to be held each year.[31] Unfortunately, due to political reasons, the dialogue initiative was terminated in 2011.[32]

The Azhari *Majalla* journal features only very few and short reports of visits of Christian church leaders or events. In general, the idea of interreligious dialogue about theological issues does not seem to meet with much approval by Muslims, since many believe that they already know all about Christians from reading the Qur'an. This is a common argument. Another argument commonly found is that Christians must first cease their mission efforts and must stop insulting Muḥammad (yet no explanation is provided as to what that is supposed to mean) before any dialogue can take place.[33]

In his book, Hussein Hamdan claims that al-Azhar is an important dialogue partner. The findings of his book do not however prove this claim. On the contrary, it would seem that Al-Azhar is important rather because of its reputation within the Muslim world and because of its size, not because of its efforts. After all, almost no such efforts have taken place at all. Hamdan seeks to prove his claim in his book, but he often ends up turning to topics such as the Regensburg Address of the Pope, the cartoon controversy, and others, since there clearly is not much to write about dialogue on the part of al-Azhar.

2.2.3. Aḥmad Muḥammad aṭ-Ṭayyib (Grand Sheikh 2010-)

Under the new Grand Sheikh Aḥmad Muḥammad aṭ-Ṭayyib, al-Azhar seems to have begun promoting interfaith activities with special attention to the Egyptian context. A forum was started for this purpose, called *House of the Egyptian Family* or simply *Family House* (*bait al-'ā'ila al-Miṣrīya* in Arabic). After violent attacks had been carried out on Christian churches in Iraq, with hostages being taken and killed, the Grand Sheikh decided to set up a forum on interfaith relations in order to work against extremist tendencies in Egypt. The forum was initiated by representatives of al-Azhar in 2011. It is comprised of Azharis as well as of representatives of the Coptic Orthodox Church, the Protestant Churches, the Catholic Church, and the Anglican Church, plus a number of scholars of sociology, history, and cultural studies from both sides. The forum is chaired by the Grand Sheikh of al-Azhar and the pope of the Coptic Orthodox Church, each of whom is repre-

29 Hamdan, *Dialog*, 253.
30 Hamdan, *Dialog*, 161.
31 Hamdan, *Dialog*, 252-255.
32 Hamdan, *Dialog*, 292-300.
33 Hamdan, *Dialog*, 239.

sented by a general secretary. The forum regards itself an independent commission of national importance, financed by the aforementioned religious bodies. Grants offered by the government are not accepted by the forum, since it prefers to avoid the impression that it speaks on behalf the government.

What are the aims of the forum? Firstly, the forum aims to improve the manner in which and the *rhetoric by which* media speak about issues touching on Muslim-Christian relations, and to eliminate hate speech as much as possible. A second goal of the forum is *to distinguish whether* incidents or social phenomena can be attributed to religious matters or not. Far too many phenomena associated with day-to-day politics are viewed by the media and in public opinion *through a religious lens*, and so the challenge is to de-mystify such reports and discourses. Many problems and incidents cannot be traced back to an underlying religious cause, but arise simply from underdeveloped social assistance, weak healthcare, corruption, poverty, illiteracy, and other such factors. By means of research carried out by social scientists, the forum aims to highlight the real problems behind issues that are all too frequently attributed in the media and in public opinion to religious groups, group interests, and the like. Thirdly, the forum seeks to meet the need for proper documentation of incidents like bombings, killings, or uprisings, and to conduct research on the reasons behind such violent acts.

In short, this forum represents a kind of social dialogue in its own right, since it is not simply an attempt to bring people together to cooperate for the good of the region, but to conduct joint research (by Christians, Muslims, and social scientists) on problems, incidents, and challenges in order to identify the real issues behind the phenomena in question. Naturally, the tasks of the forum imply the need for a critical view of the shortcomings of all sides, but this applies first and foremost to the shortcomings of the government, since the government far too often fails in providing social care, medical treatment, schooling, and other state services, with the result that social tensions arise not primarily because of religious conflicts, but because of a lack of resources. These tensions can be used all too easily by extremists for purposes of stirring up hatred between different religious groups; conversely, it is just as easy for the media to blame social tensions on religious sentiments, even when this is clearly not the case. The forum undoubtedly is a valuable enterprise. Its concern is *not* theological issues between Muslims and Christians; rather, the forum is concerned with the *religious lenses* of different actors, be they from the Muslim or the Christian side.[34]

2.2.4. Maḥmūd Ḥamdī Zaqzūq (Minister of Religious Affairs 1996-2011)

Throughout the period in which these three Grand Sheikhs have been in office, another Azhari was also of great importance for Muslim-Christian relations in Egypt: From 1987 to 1995, Maḥmūd Zaqzūq was in charge of the *Faculty of Islamic Theology* at al-Azhar University, and from 1996 until 2011, he also headed up the

[34] Hamdan, *Dialog*, 315-320.

ministry of religious affairs of the Egyptian government.[35] In 1994, an article on dialogue was published in *Majallat al-Azhar*, written mainly by Zaqzūq. Zaqzūq was well equipped to write on dialogue, since he had studied philosophy in Germany and holds a doctoral degree from the University of Munich.

The article argues that while dialogues should be held on social matters and specific values affirmed by different religions, they should however not be held on matters of belief or creed. In the text, Zaqzūq affirms that the dialogue should be premised on a sense of equality between the participants, and furthermore, that there should be a clear purpose and goal to the dialogue, as well as an appropriate framework for conducting the dialogue. Zaqzūq states that for Muslims, it is necessary for interreligious dialogue patently to be based on principles stipulated in the Qur'an. Muslims should come together with others for a common word (Surah 3:64), argue in the best manner (Surah 29:46), invite others to Islam (Surah 16:125), and attempt to get to know and recognize other people (Surah 49:13). Furthermore, Muslims should respect religious differences (Surah 109:6), not compel anybody in matters of religion (Surah 2:256), and work for the common good.[36]

With this understanding, Zaqzūq is clearly opting for social dialogue based on Islamic theological principles derived from various Qur'anic passages. By taking this approach, he avoids the comparison of religions altogether. Since the article in the *Majalla* is the most comprehensive text on the subject of dialogue written by a high-ranking Islamic religious official in Egypt, it supplies the most unambiguous evidence of the Islamic preference for a dialogue that brackets religious differences.

2.3. Al-Azhar Scholars and the Role of Islamic Intellectuals in Egypt

Having completed this basic overview, some remarks concerning the role of Islamic intellectuals in a society like Egypt are in order. In public debates in Egypt and other Muslim majority countries, it is very common for religious scholars and leaders to speak up and take a stance. Unlike in the West, religious scholars here do not confine themselves to a rather narrow field of studies in order to show their expertise in that particular field. On the contrary, in majority Muslim contexts, religious scholars often opt to speak to a wide audience by using phraseology and arguments that can easily be grasped, even by poorly educated people. Therefore the role of intellectuals in these contexts is different from their counterparts in Western countries. It is important to take this difference into account and to bear it in mind in order to understand the texts to be analyzed in the next section of this study. Western readers might be tempted to think that a lot of arguments given in the texts are rather basic, if not overly simple. How can people regarded as

[35] Hamdan, *Dialog*, 153-160.

[36] Hamdan, *Dialog*, 154-159. Mahmoud Zakzouk, "Der Dialog zwischen den drei monotheistischen Religionen aus islamischer Sicht," in id., *Einführung in den Islam* (Kairo: Ministerium für Religiöse Stiftungen, 2000), 387-400.

scholars argue in such simple ways? The answer (at least in part) is that the more people who understand an argument, the more impact it has; it is the number of followers that gives a voice its weight. In other words, the more people follow the opinion of a particular scholar, the more his opinion counts in the public debate. Concomitantly, the simpler the argument, the more potential followers it attracts. This is not to say that all utterances by scholars are aimed at describing issues in ordinary ways; but this phenomenon does help Westerners understand why – even in religious matters – the intellectual level of a text written by one or the other scholar might be rather basic.

With that being said, we are now ready to turn to a selection of books by al-Azhar scholars on Christianity and the Christian faith and creeds. Our question will be: How do they conduct the comparison of religions? How do they regard Christianity, Christian scriptures, and Christian creeds? How do they define the relations between Islam and Christianity?

3. Al-Azhar Scholars and Other Islamic Authors on Christ and Christianity

It has already been noted that al-Azhar University has widespread influence in Egyptian society, and that the statements of al-Azhar officials are of importance for Egyptian society and sometimes for the wider world of Sunni Islam as well. Now what is taught at al-Azhar University about adherents of other religions? To answer this question, we turn to the work of al-Azhar scholars who have contributed to the topic of the comparison of religions.

3.1. Voices from the 1950s up until Today

3.1.1. Muḥammad Abū Zahra

Islamic authors who take what might be labeled an *apologetical approach* seek to convince their readers that Islam is the only valid religious option and that other religions have deviated from the straight path and the true religion. In this respect, a groundbreaking book was published by Muḥammad Abū Zahra under the title *Lectures on Christianity* (*Muhadarat fi'l-Nasraniyya* in Arabic).[1] The first edition appeared in 1942, but new editions have been continually published since then.

Hugh Goddard quotes Azhari scholar Dr. Ahmad Ghalwash as saying that this book has served as "the basis for every other book on the subject published since."[2] Muḥammad Abū Zahra was lecturer at al-Azhar's *College of the Principles of Religion* (*Uṣūl ad-dīn* in Arabic). This college falls under the *Department of the Call to Islam and Guidance* (*ad-da'wah wa-l irshād* in Arabic). Abū Zahra's book is a collection of his lectures on the topic. The content mainly comprises a historical overview of the development of Christian doctrine. The author claims that his goal is to deal with the topic in an unbiased and scholarly manner, to use only Christian sources, and to depict Christian doctrines as understood by Christians themselves. However, the work patently does not live up to these claims. Abū Zahra's main thesis is that between the time of Jesus and the time of the ancient church councils,

[1] Muḥammad Abū Zahra, *Muhadarat fi'l-Nasraniyya* (1942, repr. Cairo: Dar al-Fikr al-Arabi, 1961); Hugh Goddard, *Muslim Perceptions of Christianity* (London: Grey Seal, 1996), 60-67.

[2] Goddard, *Muslim Perceptions*, 60.

Christians deviated from the original message of Jesus, and that masses of converts with a pagan background who flooded into the church in the third and fourth centuries altered the message and introduced pagan ideas. Contrary to the author's stated intent of using only Christian sources, it must be noted that he mainly uses Islamic sources, largely quotations from the Qur'an, to interpret what he believes to be original Christian teachings; in fact, all of Abū Zahra's sources on Christianity are secondary sources.

Goddard notes:

> Abu Zahra's main sources of reference are in fact Ibn Hazm and Rahmat Allah al-Hindi's Izhar al-haqq (Demonstration of truth). Thus despite claims of being scientific and the use of original sources, Abu Zahra is in reality limited to Arabic sources, and demonstrates a considerable reliance on traditional Muslim anti-Christian polemic. It is, therefore, the traditional Muslim picture of Jesus and Christianity which emerges from the pages of this book.[3]

Small wonder, then, that Abū Zahra rejects the Christian understanding of the crucifixion of Christ, the doctrine of the incarnation, the Trinity, and many other Christian teachings. As mentioned, Abū Zahra's main source is Ibn Ḥazm, a medieval writer. Goddard states that Ibn Ḥazm's "influence on subsequent writers is rather diffused, in that it has become part of the accepted wisdom on Christianity."[4] In the decades following the 1950s, not only was the book by Abū Zahra reprinted no less than five times, but reprints of Ibn Ḥazm's *Izhar al-haqq* were also published. One edition was produced by Muḥammad Kamal Farag in 1978 with a preface by 'Abd al-Ḥalīm Maḥmūd, who served as Grand Sheikh of al-Azhar from 1973 to 1978. Such an affirmation by a high-ranking al-Azhar official shows that he was in full agreement with the content of *Izhar al-haqq*. The editor of the other 1970s edition of *Izhar al-haqq* was Ahmad Hijazi al-Saqqa.

3.1.2. Aḥmad Hijazi al-Saqqa

Aḥmad Hijazi al-Saqqa was educated at al-Azhar and holds a doctoral degree from the *College of the Principles of Religion*. His doctoral dissertation was entitled *The Annunciation of the Prophet of Islam in the Torah and the Injil.* Goddard observes that al-Saqqa is a "prolific author" who wrote many books, while "much of the material in his other books is ultimately derived from this book," meaning *Izhar al-haqq*. Therefore al-Saqqa had a vested interest in repristinating *Izhar al-haqq* as proof of his usage of and quotations from this particular book.[5] Al-Saqqa regards *Izhar al-haqq* as the "first book of Muslim comparative religion."[6] According to him, a number of authors used this book intensively for their own work – authors

---

[3] Goddard, *Muslim Perceptions*, 62.

[4] Goddard, *Muslim Perceptions*, 67.

[5] Goddard, *Muslim Perceptions*, 70.

[6] As quoted in Goddard, *Muslim Perceptions*, 71.

like Rashīd Riḍā, Muḥammad al-Ghazālī, Ḥasan Ḥanafī, and Muḥammad ‘Izat Ismā‘īl al-Ṭahṭāwī.[7] This shows the importance of writers from other periods of time like the Middle Ages for Muslim writers of today.

In his own works like the book *Aqanim al-nasara* (1977),[8] al-Saqqa repeatedly states that Christian doctrine was corrupted during the first centuries after Jesus.[9] Al-Saqqa mentions that he decided to write a book on this topic after he had read a book by Elias Maqar, a theologian of the Coptic Evangelical Church, entitled *My Faith* (*Imani* in Arabic). After reviewing *Aqanim al-nasara* and another book by al-Saqqa, *Goddard* concludes:

> Al-Saqqa's published works are... somewhat repetitive, both of each other and of earlier works, particularly Izhar al-haqq. Since he is described by many, however, as being Egypt's leading expert on Christianity, it is important that his views be understood. His particular contribution to recent Muslim writing about Christianity has been his detailed work on prophecies of Muhammad, and it is significant that a number of authors have taken up this same theme in recent years.[10]

One may summarize that authors following al-Saqqa's line of thinking are mainly concerned with using Biblical sources as proofs for the coming of the prophet Muḥammad. This is meant to convince adherents of Judaism and Christianity to convert to Islam. This line of argument is seen as a proper method of comparative religion. Goddard notes with regard to al-Saqqa and Abū Zahra:

> Comparative religion is thus clearly seen as being one particular way of examining another religious tradition and yet at the same time a vigorous assertion of the superiority of the religion of the writer, and indeed of the correctness of the claim of his religion to surpass and supplant the religious tradition about which he is writing.[11]

3.1.3. Muḥammad Kamil Husain

Besides books on Christianity written by al-Azhar scholars, a number of either biographical or fictional works about Jesus have also been published. This is a different genre of literature and will be touched on only briefly. Important and well-known works on Jesus are books like *City of Wrong* by Muḥammad Kamil Husain and *The Genius of Christ* by ‘Abbas Mahmud al-‘Aqqad. Goddard holds the book of Muḥammad Kamil Husain to be the “most famous Egyptian book on the subject of Christianity”[12] written from the 1960s on. Spatial limitations prevent

[7] Goddard, *Muslim Perceptions*, 71.

[8] Al-Saqqa, Ahmad Hijazi, *Aqanim al-Nasara* (Cairo: Dar al-Ansar, 1977).

[9] Goddard, *Muslim Perceptions*, 76-79.

[10] Goddard, *Muslim Perceptions*, 83.

[11] Goddard, *Muslim Perceptions*, 83.

[12] Goddard, *Muslim Perceptions*, 98.

us from pursuing this topic in depth here. A few remarks concerning Muḥammad Kamil Husain's *City of Wrong* will need to suffice.

In 1957, the book *City of Wrong* won the Egyptian state prize of literature. The book deals with the events that took place in Jerusalem on Good Friday. It is not concerned with historical details, but with the question as to what the intention and motivation of the people were in letting Jesus be crucified by the Romans. Goddard writes:

> So the book is really about sin, about humans and their desire and ability to do evil; and more particularly it is about communal sin, and the ability of people in a group to do what they know individually to be wrong. Indeed it has been suggested that the book's main concern is with consensus (ijma'), for it was by consensus that Jesus was crucified, despite the fact that most of the individuals who made up that consensus knew in their own minds that what was going to happen was wrong. So the book is at root an examination of humanity's hopes and fears, conscience and ability to stifle it, for it is conscience that Husain sees as the guiding light for humanity.[13]

Goddard finds that there are basic differences between the approach taken by biographies and that taken by fictional literature, inasmuch as *biographies* – in line with Islamic tradition – concentrate on Jesus as a teacher, whereas *fictional literature* depicts Jesus not only as a teacher, but also using the trope of the *rejected sufferer*, an trope that might best be understood with regard to the political circumstances of the repression during the reign of al-Nāṣīr. This topic, however, emphasizes an aspect that has seldomly been touched on in Muslim tradition. Goddard: "Most of the authors who see the Cross in a positive light, however, still do so within what is a fundamentally Islamic framework. The symbol of the Cross is used, in other words, to illustrate essentially Islamic themes."[14]

Biographical and fictional books on Jesus tend to be rather positive in their approach, even though they remain in line with Islamic orthodoxy. At any rate, their overall intention is not to refute Christian understandings of Jesus. According to Goddard it is for "the future... perhaps the fictional appreciation of the significance of the crucified Jesus which has the most potential for furthering Muslim understanding of Christianity. ... Other types of writing about Christianity, however, also continue to be produced."[15]

3.1.4. Maḥmūd Abū Rayya

In the year 1970, a book by Maḥmūd Abū Rayya, an Azhari scholar, was published under the title *Din allah wahid – muhammad wa'l-masih akhawan*. After encountering some criticism, the second edition appeared under a different title, *Din allah*

[13] Goddard, *Muslim Perceptions*, 97.

[14] Goddard, *Muslim Perceptions*, 140.

[15] Goddard, *Muslim Perceptions*, 140.

wahid - 'ala alsina jami' al-rusul.[16] The intent of the author Maḥmūd Abū Rayya is to prove that according to human reason, God must be one and that religion must be one and the same, irrespective of minor differences. The argument goes as follows: Since all religions are essentially one, their adherents should seek to cooperate. Adherents of one religion should not claim that their religion is better than that of the others, because this would stir up enmity. Instead, both should focus on the common basis. Now for Abū Rayya, this basis is without doubt Islam in the sense that all religions stem from the one original religion. Therefore he reasons that adherents of other religions should return to the original teaching, since by doing so, the differences between the religions could be overcome. Since this original religion, which is essentially Islam, is common to all human beings, there is no need for a special religious status. Therefore baptism, for instance, is obsolete. According to Abū Rayya, there also can be no such thing as vicarious suffering on the part of Christ.

Goddard concludes that the book is "essentially a plea for good relationships between Christians and Muslims, rather than an attempt at promoting the understanding of Christianity."[17] Whereas Abū Rayya seems to concede a certain validity to Christianity, he rejects Christian content like the doctrines of the incarnation, crucifixion, vicarious suffering, or Trinity. We may conclude that while Azhari scholars like *Abū Rayya* or *Mahmūd Zaqzūq* initially seem more openminded than authors like *Abū Zahra* or *al-Saqqa*, the positive attitude towards Christianity ultimately turns out to be very limited, and the claim to the finality and superiority of Islam as the original and pure religion prevails.

3.2. Different Approaches – An Overview

Goddard differentiates between three general approaches taken by al-Azhar scholars with regard to other religions, namely the *apologetic* (or polemical) *approach*, the *eirenical approach*, and the *intermediate approach*. This is a useful framework, even though it does not speak to the methodology applied by various authors. The question we are concerned with here is how exactly does the comparison of religions function in the work of Azhari and other authors? In the next part of this study, we will turn to three present-day Azhari scholars who claim to engage in the comparison of religions. Our aim will be to analyze their way of thinking and the way they make use of Islamic sources, on the one hand, and of resources of other religions (specifically, of Christianity) on the other. My conviction is that if Azhari scholars were willing to interpret the Christian faith, doctrines, and creed within the framework of Christian thinking, they would then also be able to admit that the Christian faith, doctrines, and creed are a coherent structure. They could then take issue with this structure, given that Muslims would never agree to the axioms

---

[16] Muḥammad Abū Rayya, *Din allah wahid – muhammad wa'l-masih akhawan* (Cairo: Dar al-karnak, 1963); id., *Din allah wahid – 'ala alsina jami' al rusul.* 2nd ed. (Cairo: Alam al-kutub, 1970).

[17] Goddard, *Muslim Perceptions*, 162.

of Christian thinking. The first step in this direction would be to concede that the Christian faith, doctrines, and creed are not irrational, blasphemous, or mere phantasy. If Muslims would at least grant that Christians follow a theological logic that is coherent in its own right, then they could appreciate the *otherness of the Other* without agreeing to the faith itself. This in itself would be an important step.

We now turn to the work of the first of our three Azhari scholars, Maḥmūd 'Alī Ḥimāiyah.

Part II.

Islamic Azhari Scholars on the Comparison of Religions

In the preceding chapters, we have analyzed the situation in Egypt with regard to Muslim-Christian relations. It has become clear that even today, dialogue initiatives play a minor role, whereas the discourse on national unity continues to dominate. We have reflected on different perspectives on the issue, highlighting the fact that when considering interfaith relations, power relations always have to be taken into account as well. With regard to power relations, the high regard in which institutions like al-Azhar University are held is unquestionably important. Recalling the demand of Muḥammad Abū-Nimer that in future, both Muslims and Christians should be better and more comprehensively informed about the faith of the Other, we now turn to scholars of al-Azhar University particularly concerned with the comparison of religions, that is, with providing information on the sources, faith, and practices of the religious Other. The point of inquiry is: How do these scholars undertake the comparison of religions? What kind of methodology do they apply? With what aim are such comparisons carried out? Is there an attempt to understand the religious Other on her own terms and in her own framework? Does the methodology of comparison contribute to a better understanding of, and, concomitantly, to a greater appreciation for the religious Other?

4. Maḥmūd 'Alī 'Abdel Raḥmān Ḥimāiyah

Our object of study in this chapter is a recent book by Dr. Maḥmūd 'Alī Ḥimāiyah. Ḥimāiyah served as professor at al-Azhar University and as head of the *Comparison of Religions Department* (*muqārnat al-adyān* in Arabic) at the Assiut, Upper Egypt branch of al-Azhar University. His book is available in many bookstores in Egypt. It was published in 2005. In this chapter, our aim is to analyze Ḥimāiyah's approach to the comparison of religions in his book. In preparation for that analysis, some biographical information on Ḥimāiyah is in order.

4.1. Introduction

4.1.1. Biography

Maḥmūd 'Alī 'Abdel Raḥmān Ḥimāiyah was born on May 25, 1946 in Musha, a little village in the province of Assiut, Upper Egypt. He grew up in a religious Islamic family. He was able to recite the entire Qur'an at an early age already. In 1960, he enrolled in the Assiut religious institute and spent a total of nine years there, four years in the preparatory stage and five years in the secondary stage. In 1969, he obtained the secondary certificate of al-Azhar. At this point, he enrolled in the *Faculty of the Fundamentals of Religion* (*kullīyat uṣūl ad-dīn* in Arabic) in Assiut. At that time, it was being headed up by Dr. Muḥammad Abū Shahba. Ḥimāiyah states that he had great appreciation for his dean, saying that Abū Shahba was a defender of the *Sunnah* of the prophet Muḥammad. In 1973, a few months after finishing his BA, Ḥimāiyah was appointed as a lecturer at al-Azhar. Concurrently, he enrolled in postgraduate studies as a master's student at al-Azhar University in Cairo, where he received an MA in 1975.

In 1980, he obtained a doctorate in comparative religions. His thesis dealt with a book of *Ibn Ḥazm Andalusi*, who died in the year 1064. Afterwards, he continued his research and studies in Cairo. He was appointed as a lecturer in the *Faculty of the Fundamentals of Religion* in Assiut in 1981 and was promoted to assistant professor in 1985. In 1990, he was appointed head of the *Department of Islamic Da'wah* (call) *and Culture* in the *Faculty of the Fundamentals of Religion* in Assiut. From 1995 to 1997, he served as professor of comparative religions at the *International Islamic University of Islamabad* in Pakistan. After returning to Egypt, he served as head of the *Comparison of Religions Department* (*muqārnat al-adyān* in Arabic) at al-Azhar University in Assiut, Upper Egypt. During the

1990s, Ḥimāiyah also taught at *Umm al Quraa University* in Saudi Arabia for a spell.

Ḥimāiyah published a number of books mostly dealing with the comparison between Islam and Christianity.[1] Among these is the book *Trinity between Paganism and Christianity* (*tat̲līt̲ bayna al-wat̲anīya wa al-masīḥīya* in Arabic). In addition to his academic teaching, he also published articles in Egyptian newspapers, defending Islam against what he saw as secularism, atheism, communism, and other worldviews.

4.1.2. Tat̲līt̲: A Comparison between Islam and Christianity – On Ḥimāiyah's Methodology

The author begins with some methodological remarks that clearly show what he understands *comparative religion* to mean. He states:

> This is the seventh book in a series on the field of comparative religion that I present to the reader in an easy way. I order the evidence and the arguments and proceed by way of scholarly investigation, drawing on the most correct and documented sources. Our book deals with the doctrine of Trinity on the basis of Christian sources and holy books. I try to present them carefully and honestly, without going beyond them or misrepresenting their beliefs. The earnest reader will find in this research the evidence and proofs that illuminate the way for him to know the truth and to attain it. I do not want to write a conclusion on the content of this book in this introduction. ... It is better to let the reader himself discover the truth, in order to enable him to exercise by himself the right to accept or reject it. And Allah guides whom he wills to a straight path.[2]

The author claims that his work takes the form of a *scholarly investigation* (*taḥqīq 'ilmī* in Arabic). The term "scholarly" here means that the author provides *evidence* (*'adila* in Arabic) and *arguments (ḥujaj* in Arabic) on the basis of

---

[1] These include (names provided in English translation): 1) Method of Ibn Ḥazm in the Study of Religions; 2) Masterpiece of the Areeb in Response to the People of the Cross to the Converted Priest Anselm Tormida (Submission, Investigation, and Study); 3) Study of the Bible (Old and New Testament); 4) Trinity (*tat̲līt̲* in Arabic) between Paganism and Christianity; 5) Christian Worship (a critical study); 6) Incarnation and Crucifixion between Truth and Slander; 7) The Grand Debate between Sheikh Ahmed Deedat and Rev. Jimmy Swaggart (Presentation, Comment, and Study); 8) The Approach of Abraham (Peace Be upon Him) in the Da'wah (call) to God; 9) Lectures in Islamic Systems; 10) The Path of Guidance in the Da 'wah (call) and Guidance. Most of these books are published by *Dar al-Ma'arif* in Cairo.

[2] Maḥmūd 'Alī 'Abdel Raḥmān Ḥimāiyah, *Tat̲līt̲ bayna al-wat̲anīya wa al-masīḥīya* (Cairo: Dar al-Ma'arif, 2005), preface (no numbering provided). I should clarify that all English translations of Arabic originals, unless drawn from cited published translations, are my own as someone fluent in both Arabic and English.

the original (in this case: Christian) *sources*. The author furthermore states that he has tried to avoid going beyond or misrepresenting the Christian sources. This kind of neutral presentation of the material is, according to the author, an important *precondition* for readers to be able to discover the *truth* by themselves.

This passage makes the goal of the comparison clear: The goal is to find the truth. The author is therefore convinced that *there is* a truth that can be found by comparing the arguments of different religions using human reason. His reasoning is expressly predicated upon two factors: firstly, upon the fair presentation of arguments, and, secondly, upon the freedom to use one's own reasoning. According to Ḥimāiyah, then, the comparison of religions will inevitably lead to *conclusions* about the truth. He therefore believes that the comparison of religions is less about understanding a religious idea in its own framework, and more about comparing different ideas by way of human reasoning. He is not aiming at a deeper understanding of Christian doctrine, but his interest is limited to questions of logic. His method of comparison serves the attempt to distinguish between what is true and what is false.

Interestingly, the author ends this introductory passage on methodology with a quote from the Qur'an, saying that God will guide people to a straight path. It is likely that the idea behind this quotation is the Muslim understanding of Islam as a *religion of nature* (*dīn al-fiṭra* in Arabic). In many books written by Muslim authors, Islam is depicted as a natural religion and as a reasonable religion, since if God has created the world, and if God is a rational God, then the world must be rational in its very essence. Religion therefore must correspond to this rationality, and any religion that does not do so is thereby shown to be false. It would appear that the author follows this line of thinking.

4.1.3. Ḥimāiyah's Argumentation – An Overview

It is difficult to follow the author's main line of thinking, because the book does not provide a clear systematic outline. Firstly, the author covers two Christian approaches in treating and explaining the Trinitarian faith. In this first part, the author refers to various Christian sources like Augustine or present-day Christian pastors in Egypt. Secondly (pp. 14 and following), under the heading "the Christian '*Persons*'" (*āqānīm an-naṣāra* in Arabic), the author tries to describe what the New Testament scriptures (mainly the Gospels of Mark, Matthew, Luke, and John) say about God the Father, Son, and Holy Spirit, and what Christian theologians have made out of such statements. In this second part, Ḥimāiyah refers both to Biblical sources and to some Qur'anic verses. Thirdly (on pages 63 and following), the author under the heading "The Bright Proofs of the Invalidity of the Doctrine of the Trinity" (*al-barahīn sāṭ'a fī ibṭāl 'aqīdat at-taṯlīṯ* in Arabic) engages in a general refutation of the Christian doctrines of the divinity of Christ and of the Trinity. In the final chapter, entitled "The Trinitarian Doctrine and Paganism" (*'aqīdat at-taṯlīṯ wa ṯānīya* in Arabic), the author attempts to prove that the doctrine of the Trinity is pagan.

4.2. The First Line of Argument – Trinity Either as a Metaphor Or as a Mystery

As mentioned above, the author begins his discussion of Christian doctrines by stating that Christians mainly use two different ways to speak about the Trinity. The first way of the Christians, he says, is the use of metaphors to explain what the doctrine of the Trinity is supposed to mean. The second way, he argues, is for Christians to claim that the mystery of the Trinity surpasses the capabilities of human reason.

4.2.1. The Christian Use of Metaphors to Explain the Trinity

At this point, Ḥimāiyah refers not to Biblical texts but to various Christian sources. He quotes a few examples of Christian thinkers using different metaphors to explain the Trinity. In doing so, his aim is to show that these metaphors are actually not suitable to explain Christian doctrine. The metaphors are the following: Trinity as *bone, flesh, and blood*; as *body, soul, and spirit*; as *root, stump, and flower*; as *sun, rays, and heat;* and as *memory, knowledge, and love*. In discussing these examples, the author again and again attempts to show that each given metaphor covers either the meaning of an independent entity or the meaning of relatedness.

The author starts with the statement that the equation of $1 + 1 + 1 = 1$ contradicts the basic principles of logic and therefore human reason itself. Nevertheless, he argues, Christians have often tried to explain the Trinity as composed of three entities while at the same time claiming that these entities are one.

4.2.1.1. Ḥimāiyah's Discussion of Metaphors

Ḥimāiyah's argumentation revolves around the question of how something can be composed of different elements while at the same time, these elements are said to be independent of each other. He endeavors to show that all metaphors used by Christian thinkers are insufficient. Ḥimāiyah begins by referring to an Egyptian Pastor, Kaim Eldeen Said, who used the example of bone, flesh, and blood. The human body needs all three of them, but a human body can only live when it is a unified whole. The author argues against this metaphor in that it speaks of three parts of the body, whereas Christian doctrine holds that the three persons of God are not be thought of as "parts." This, according to the author, also holds true for the metaphors of body, soul, and spirit, and of root, stump, and flower. His main argument is that these metaphors fail to explain how elements can be both unified and at the same time independent from each other.

With reference to Girgis Habib (see below), the author goes on to argue that the metaphor of sun, rays, and heat, used by Habib, cannot explain the aspect of independence, since heat and rays are not independent from the sun. According to the author, the strongest metaphor for the Trinity was that proposed by the church father Augustine. It is the metaphor of one who knows – the union of memory, knowledge, and love. But, once again, Ḥimāiyah argues that this metaphor is not able to explain the independence of the three elements claimed to be one entity.

4.2.1.2. Quoting from Christian Sources

In this first section, the author refers to Augustine, yet he does not deal with the thinking of Augustine, but only gives a very brief quotation from his works.

He also refers to Girgis Habib, who was a prominent figure of the Coptic Orthodox Church. Habib lived from 1876 until 1951. He is considered to be the founder of the Coptic Orthodox Seminary. Furthermore, he was active in the Sunday school movement and wrote a number of books on topics like hymns, poetry, spirituality, and doctrine. Even though he was an influential leader, his formal qualification was rather low, since he did not study at a university. Girgis Habib was a layperson who was never ordained. Ordination would have required a specific theological qualification.

The third person the author refers to is Pastor Kaim Eldeen Said.

4.2.1.3. The Intention behind the Comparison

It is important to note that Ḥimāiyah does not begin his book by examining the New Testament or the four gospels in particular, but by dealing with the question of the attributes of God. This is a typical Islamic approach, since Muslim doctrinal debates from the early times on were concerned with the question of how the oneness of God can be thought of, and furthermore, whether the attributes of God are something separate beside the entity of the one God. Therefore, the author – thus far, at any rate – does not try to understand the basic assumptions of Christian theological reflection. Instead, he adheres to an Islamic approach in that he mainly addresses the question as to what might be attributed to God as a transcendent entity.

4.2.2. The Doctrine of the Trinity as a Mystery

Ḥimāiyah then goes on to assert that some Christians in and of themselves believe that human beings are unable to comprehend the mystery of the Trinity. To prove his assertions, he quotes Muslim authorities like al-Jāḥiẓ, ar-Rāzī, and Ibn Taymiyya. In his conclusion, the author gives his own opinion concerning Christian theologians whom he simply calls "bishops." Ḥimāiyah states:

> This fact has been recognized by the bishops of the Trinity themselves and by the greatest of theologians and philosophers of Christianity as well. Even though they have to defend the doctrine of the Trinity and try to justify it to simple, ordinary people, deep down they feel their hypocrisy of reason and logic, and that it goes beyond right and truth. We find that these Christian theologians and philosophers often recognize this reality and respond to the screams of their minds, which, being created, are by nature monotheistic and cannot put up with the Trinity.[3]

---

[3] Ḥimāiyah, *Taṯlīṯ*, 10 (Ḥimāiyah here refers to a quote by Muḥammad Majda, but provides no source).

In this statement, Ḥimāiyah alleges that Christian theologians, while adhering to the doctrine of the Trinity, sense within themselves that this doctrine contradicts human reasoning. His argument is that according to Islamic tradition, in creating human beings, God also gave them reason. By creating human beings, God has also endowed then with the sense that there is only one God. This line of thinking is taken from the Qur'an, where God after the creation of man asks him whom he should serve. Even though this Qur'anic passage is not quoted here, it is obvious that this is the underlying principle.

4.3. The Second Line of Argument – Father, Son, and Holy Spirit

Under the heading "Why Three Persons?,"[4] the author attempts to refute the overall claim of Christians by stating, firstly, that the books of the Old and New Testaments are full of contradictions; secondly, that it is a trick of Christian authors to read the divinity of Christ into the texts; and, thirdly, that this is all manipulation and heresy. After this attempted refutation, the author then deals at length with the topics of the Father (p. 23), the Son (pp. 23 ff.), and the Holy Spirit (pp. 46 ff.).

4.3.1. Refutation of the Christian Claim That Christ Is the Son of God

In this section, Ḥimāiyah deals separately with the three persons of Father, Son, and Holy Spirit. It is interesting that he deals with the Son and Holy Spirit at length, but speaks of the Father only very briefly. We will return to this observation later on.

4.3.1.1. Remarks Concerning the Father

Concerning God the Father, Ḥimāiyah briefly states that:

> for Christians, the Father is the divine self alone, apart from the two attributes of the word and the life, in that He is the origin and the principle of the existence of the Son. That does not mean that the Father gave birth to someone or that there was a long time when the Father was alone without the Son; rather, it is a theological term that means that the Father is the only principle of the Son, as the self is the principle of the attributes. Otherwise, the Son has existed since the Father has existed as well, and there was not a time when one of them preceded the other.[5]

---

[4] Ḥimāiyah, *Taṯlīṯ,* 20ff.

[5] Ḥimāiyah, *Taṯlīṯ*, 23.

Ḥimāiyah attests this claim with a footnote that mentions a book on Thomas Aquinas.

He then proceeds:

> And why is the divine Self called Father? In answer to this question, Alfred Garoudy says: "The purpose is to call attention to some facts: First, it indicates that all creatures owe their existence to God as a son does to his father. Second, it is a sign that God is gentle with His people, and His compassion toward them is the kindness a father has toward his son."[6]

For this passage, the author provides a footnote mentioning an article by Alfred Garoudy, published in *The Encyclopedia of Religions and Ethics*, vol. 3, page 585. This encyclopedia was published between 1906 and 1927, was edited by James Hastings, and comprises twelve volumes.

4.3.1.2. Remarks Concerning Christ as the Son of God

Under the heading "Why was Christ called the Son of God?" (pages 24-47), Ḥimāiyah first emphasizes that according to Christians, this title is supposed to express the *unity of nature* between Father and Son and a *similarity* between the two. In discussing this issue the author refers to the following as proof for the Islamic view: (a) a book of systematic theology; (b) utterances by Pastor Labib Michael and (c) Pastor Menis Abd Al-Nour; (d) a text from the year 1913, written by Father Louis Shiecho; and (e) a quote by Anselm Turmeda (1353-1430), a former Dominican friar who converted to Islam.[7] Compared to these few references, almost all other quotations in this chapter are from the New Testament, and especially from the four gospels. Only two references are made to the Qur'an (of which one is to Surah 112).

Ḥimāiyah argues against the Christian claim that Christ is the Son of God by explaining that in the four gospels, *believers* are called children of God, such that the question arises as to what the difference may be between believers and Christ. The author then cites Pastor Menis who argues for unity between God the Father and the Son by quoting John 10:30 and John 14:9, saying that Christ is the Son of God from the beginning, that is, from before the creation of the world, whereas Christian believers are adopted to become children of God by believing in Christ. Ḥimāiyah also quotes Father Louis Shiecho who referred to John 1:1 and John 1:14 to prove that Christ is the Son of God.

---

[6] Ḥimāiyah, *Taṯlīṯ*, 23.

[7] For more on Turmeda and his biography, see Roger Boase, "Autobiography of a Muslim Convert: Anselm Turmeda (c.1353-c.1430)," in *Al-Masāq: Studia Arabo-Islamica Mediterranea*. Vol. 9 (Leeds: Department of Modern Arabic Studies, University of Leeds, 1996/7), 45-98. Boase writes: "What is unusual about Turmeda is his double Christian-Muslim literary identity. In Muslim countries his refutation of Christianity (*Tuḥfat al-Adīb fī l-Radd ʿalā Ahl a-Salīb*) is well known. It is found in most Arab libraries." Ibid., 55-56.

He then proceeds to give a number of arguments against the divine nature of Christ. He argues that the "beginning" in John 1:1 does not necessarily mean the absolute beginning. Next, Ḥimāiyah states that the sentence "and the Word was with God, and the Word was God"[8] is a contradiction. The author asks: "Is this not clear evidence of contradiction? How can the Word be with God and be God itself?"[9] Here Ḥimāiyah's argument is premised on the logic that a thing is either to be categorized as human or divine, but it cannot be both.

The next two points against the divinity of Christ repeat rather classical Islamic arguments: The first is that Christ cannot be said to be special over against other figures, since he came into being in a way similar to Adam, that is, by God's command: "Let there be…" The only difference is that while Christ was born without a human father, Adam was born not only without a human father, but also without a human mother.

The second is that the term "son," as Ḥimāiyah claims by quoting Mark 15:39 and Luke 33:47, only means "righteous man." The comparison of these verses from the Gospel of Mark and the Gospel of Luke leads the author to conclude that the meaning of "son" must be "righteous man." Quoting a number of verses from the Old and New Testament,[10] the author goes on to conclude that Adam, Israel, David, Solomon, and others too have been called "son of God" or "children of God." Beyond that, Ḥimāiyah claims that Christ in his own words never used the phrase "Son of God," but that he spoke of "the Father" and "the Son" instead. The phrase "Son of God" was used only by others (referring to Matt. 26:63, 4:6.)

What Christ did often use was the term "Son of Man." Ḥimāiyah states: "What is really strange is that Christians abandon the title 'Son of Man,' which the Christ liked, while retaining 'Son of God.' But what was the Christ's purpose in using the title 'Son of Man' so many times?"[11] Ḥimāiyah quotes Pastor Menis as explaining that Christ used the term "Son of Man" to show his humility. He then argues against this explanation by saying that humility is not one of God's attributes, and that therefore it would be false to claim that Christ should be regarded as Son of God. Ḥimāiyah writes: "And the statement that Christ's intent with this title is humility – this is a twisted argument [*kalām fāsid* in Arabic]."[12]

Ḥimāiyah's arguments on pages 30 and following may be summarized as follows: With regard to John 15:19, Ḥimāiyah argues that "not being of this world" simply means "being a righteous and ascetic person." Furthermore, with regard to John 10:30 and John 17:21-23, he asserts that the union between Christ and the Father is not a real union, but that it is meant metaphorically, since unity with God simply means *to follow God's commands*.

Even *miracles*, as Ḥimāiyah explains with reference to John 11:38-44, are no proof of Christ's divinity because, firstly, Christ could do miracles only with per-

---

[8] In this study, the NIV will be used for all Bible quotations.

[9] Ḥimāiyah, *Taṯlīṯ*, 25.

[10] Quotations are taken from Luke 3:38; Gen. 6:2; Exod. 4:22; Ps. 89:26-27; 1 Chron. 22:10; Hosea 1:10; Matt. 5:9, 5:16, 23:9; Jer. 31:9; 2 Sam. 7:14; veiled references are also provided to Deut. 14:1, 32:19; Isa 1:2, 30:1, and 63:8.

[11] Ḥimāiyah, *Taṯlīṯ*, 29.

[12] Ḥimāiyah, *Taṯlīṯ*, 30.

mission of God,[13] and, secondly, miracles are also reported as being performed by other persons like Elijah and Moses.[14] Therefore, the author concludes, there is no difference between Christ and the other prophets. His coming into being took place by God's command: "Let there be...", just like that of all the rest of creation.[15]

Ḥimāiyah goes on to argue that the terms "God" and "Lord" are no proof of the divinity of Christ either, because these terms are used both in the Old Testament and in the New Testament. He concludes:

> Thus, if the terms "God" and "Lord" that were given to Christ necessarily make him "God," then why do Christians not say the same about Moses, Daniel, the angels, and all the other prophets? So using the terms "Lord" and "God" for Christ does not provide clear evidence that he is a partner of God!![16]

Under the heading "Evidence of the Non-divine Christ, Peace Be upon Him" (*al-'adilla 'alā 'adam al-wahīya al-masīḥ* in Arabic), Ḥimāiyah turns to Matt. 4:5-6, 10, contending that this text is an argument for the mere human nature of Christ, since Christ as God could not have been "taken away" by the devil. The author argues that since God is by definition the almighty creator, this puts paid to the notion that the devil could have "taken" Christ to Jerusalem. He states:

> This text is evidence that Christ is a human being, because if Christ is God, then Satan could not have led him to the holy city or to a high mountain to see the kingdoms of the world. Is it fitting for a God to obey the devil and go to wherever he wants? So do you think that Christ is being brought to the devil by obedience or by force?[17]

Ḥimāiyah concludes that this story can be true only if it relates to Christ as a mere human being and not as God, because it would be simply impossible for the devil to act this way with respect to God. Clearly, the author is using an axiomatic understanding of God (based upon God's attribute as being almighty) to demonstrate that this text implies that Christ's nature is that of a mere human being.

The following examples follow a similar line of reasoning: According to the Gospel of John, as Ḥimāiyah explains, Christ says that the son does not know the hour of the last day of the world, and therefore, the author concludes, the word *son* means a mere human being, since God knows all things (attribute: divine omniscience), and therefore Christ cannot be claimed to be divine.[18] Ḥimāiyah contends that the texts John 5:22, 30, 7:10, 8:28, 12:49, and 14:24, 28 serve as proof that there is no equality between God and Christ. With reference to Christ's

[13] Ḥimāiyah, *Taṯlīṯ*, 32.
[14] Ḥimāiyah, *Taṯlīṯ*, 33-34.
[15] Ḥimāiyah, *Taṯlīṯ*, 35.
[16] Ḥimāiyah, *Taṯlīṯ*, 36. *Sic.*
[17] Ḥimāiyah, *Taṯlīṯ*, 37-38.
[18] Ḥimāiyah, *Taṯlīṯ*, 39.

last days and his crucifixion, he asks why Christians still claim that there is union between God and Christ, since Christ prayed in his last hour: "My God, my God, why have you forsaken me?"[19] Furthermore, Ḥimāiyah asks to whom Christ was praying while hanging at the cross, saying: "Father, forgive them, for they do not know what they are doing."[20] He argues:

> We ask: To whom is the Christ praying if he is God, as the Christians assert? If he calls upon someone other than God, then how can he be God, seeing that he is praying to another God? This is a man being worshiped with God, yet you do not admit it. And if he is praying to himself, then this is madness...! Why not simply say: "*I* forgive you?"[21]

On the following pages, the author goes on to give one short example after the other, quoting verses from the New Testament to the effect that Christ is the *son of David* and therefore a mere human being; that the New Testament states that *God is invisible* (1 John 4:12), and therefore Christ cannot be God, because *Christ surely is visible* (attribute: invisibility of God); that God cannot cry and sweat; that John the Baptist doubted whether Jesus is the Christ; that the Trinity is not mentioned in the law of Moses; and that during his lifetime, Christ could have explained the Trinity himself.[22]

4.3.1.3. Remarks Concerning the Holy Spirit

Ḥimāiyah begins this section with information concerning the baptism of Christ, where it is reported that the Holy Spirit descended from heaven like a dove, and the author also mentions the Spirit depicted as tongues of fire coming on the disciples. He briefly refers to the discussion of the ancient church as to whether the Spirit should be understood as a power or as a person. Ḥimāiyah then proceeds to provide brief references to the Spirit as a power, as the spirit of truth and of inspiration, and as a comforter. After what amounts to only two pages of rather superficial information, the author claims: "Whoever studies the gospels seriously will find that what is said in them about the Holy Spirit is that he is only a messenger from almighty God."[23] It would seem then that the author claims to know the results of his investigation even before he has begun to examine the New Testament sources.

In what follows, the author mainly quotes from the gospel of Luke and the gospel of Matthew (especially Luke 1:15,35,41,67; 2:25-26; Matt. 1:18). His conclusion is:

> All the texts emphasize that both for us (as Muslims) and for them (as Christians), the Holy Spirit is one and the same. He is an angel from

[19] Matt. 27:46.

[20] Luke 23:34.

[21] Ḥimāiyah, *Taṯlīṯ*, 41.

[22] Ḥimāiyah, *Taṯlīṯ*, 42ff.

[23] Ḥimāiyah, *Taṯlīṯ*, 50.

> the angels of God, whose numbers no one but God can know. And concerning holiness and purification, in the gospels his counterpart is mentioned – the unclean spirit, which means Satan.[24]

Ḥimāiyah appeals to Rashid Riḍā to assert that one cannot speak of the Spirit simply as a part of God. He then asks whether, if all the disciples are said to have received the Holy Spirit, the same applies to Judas as well. This to him would be a contradiction, since Christ referred to Judas as "Satan."

Drawing on Luke 1:19, among other texts, Ḥimāiyah then again follows Riḍā in alleging that "spirit" means the angel Gabriel. With this line of reasoning, he seeks to prove that the Christian interpretation of gospel texts is incorrect. He argues that John the Baptist, Elizabeth, and others would all have to be called God or "son of God," just like the Christ, but Christians do not do so. This Ḥimāiyah labels inconsistency. "After all these many clear texts we say: It is not correct to interpret the Holy Spirit in the Christian sense that I have shown. ... Assuredly, none of the Christians talk about John or the wife of Zachariah as being divine, even though they say this of the Holy Spirit."[25]

It is interesting to note that in this passage, Ḥimāiyah admits that his own interpretation is different from that of Christians. That is to say he acknowledges the difference, but he never inquires into the reason why Christians interpret these texts differently. In so doing, the author claims that his own interpretation is the only reasonable explanation possible.

Not only does Ḥimāiyah claim that Christians distort a number of texts by imposing a wrong interpretation on them, he also goes on to contend that the text of the Gospel of John is itself distorted. According to Muslim tradition, one may distinguish between a *distortion of interpretation* (arab. *taḥrīf al-maᶜnā*) and a *distortion of the text* itself (arab. *taḥrīf al-naṣṣ*). The author clearly claims that the text of the Gospel of John is distorted, saying:

> We already mentioned that texts of the gospels use the term "Holy Spirit" as if he were an angel, however, John – the author of the fourth gospel – is the only one who wrote confused and ambiguous phrases that can be traced back to the use of others and could have been distorted [arab. taḥrīfahā] to say something else – as they have done.[26]

Having made this assertion, Ḥimāiyah proceeds to give a number of quotations from Qur'anic Surahs in order to prove that the term "spirit" means the angel Gabriel or the spirit blown into Adam after God had created him out of clay. He quotes Surahs 2:252; 5:109; 5:101; 4:170; 58:21; 66:11; 19:16; 38:71; and 21:91.

Ḥimāiyah then contends that while Christians admit that Adam was created out of clay and that God breathed his spirit into him, they would never call Adam divine, or a god, or one of the divine "persons." While the Christian understanding

[24] Ḥimāiyah, *Taṯlīṯ*, 51.

[25] Ḥimāiyah, *Taṯlīṯ*, 52.

[26] Ḥimāiyah, *Taṯlīṯ*, 52.

is complicated, the Qur'an entails a simple message that is easy to understand. The author gives a short example of a Christian doctor who converted to Islam after having received a satisfying answer from a Muslim scholar to a complicated doctrinal question.

After discussing various other issues, Ḥimāiyah avers that the term "comforter" in John 16:6-8 actually refers to Muḥammad, since this passage – according to Ḥimāiyah, at any rate – is in reality a prediction of Muḥammad's coming. Accordingly, Ḥimāiyah interprets the spirit as a *power* that strengthened all the prophets before Jesus and as an *inspiration* conveying the divine message bestowed on them. Once again the author quotes verses from various Surahs, such as Surah 53:5-6 and Surah 81:19-20. From all of this, the author draws the following conclusion:

> This indicates that both for them (as Christians) and for us (as Muslims), the Holy Spirit is one and the same. He is a strong angel who was sent down with inspiration [...] to support the messengers and prophets. We regret that the Christians, despite the abundance of evidence to the contrary, force the texts and interpret them according to another explanation that is not in accordance with human reason nor the correct revelation, and for which no warrant is found in Christ nor in the prophets of old, peace be upon them all. [...] It turns out that they – the Christians – assign to the term "Holy Spirit" a meaning beyond the one it actually has, that they attribute to it a meaning it does not have [...]. As we can see, the fact that they bestow upon the life of God the name "Holy Spirit" is something they invented and which God did not reveal to them.[27]
>
> So when it says: "baptize them in the name of the Father, the Son, and the Holy Spirit," it means: "ask the people to believe in God, in His prophet that He has sent, and in the angel with whom He sent down the inspiration upon him." This means that Christians are to believe in God, His angels, His books, and His messengers. That is the truth indicated by the reasonable use of the expression.[28]

4.3.2. Ḥimāiyah's Methodological Approach

4.3.2.1. Ḥimāiyah's Exegetical Approach

What may be said thus far about the manner in which Ḥimāiyah approaches his theme? What stands out is that he is attempting to refute what he believes to be Christian doctrines, using only quotations from the New Testament. The following may be observed:

---

[27] Ḥimāiyah, *Taṯlīṯ*, 60.

[28] Ḥimāiyah, *Taṯlīṯ*, 63.

(1) *Form*: In regard to form, Ḥimāiyah raises questions, quotes short verses from the sources, and then gives his explanation. This gives rise to a considerable number of short questions and short answers. Contrary to other scholars, the author avoids quoting verses from the Qur'an as proof for his claims, since it is his intention to refute Christian doctrines by using sources from the Christian scriptures.

(2) *Quotation of sources*: From the beginning, the author clearly shows that his intention is to refute and to correct Christian teachings. Not a single prooftext among the New Testament quotations is interpreted from within its own context. Quotations from the Gospel of John, for instance, are always taken as proof that Ḥimāiyah's own argument is correct. The storyline of the Gospel of John is omitted, as are the storylines of the other three gospels.

(3) *Use of sources*: If there are texts that seem to confirm the divine nature of Christ, the author uses one quotation to explain the other. Since the quotations are given without their context within a particular gospel, it is easy for Ḥimāiyah to support his own claims. This can be shown by an example. Ḥimāiyah quotes Mark 15:39, where the Roman centurion says: "Surely this man was the Son of God!" Next, he quotes Luke 23:47, where the centurion says: "Surely this was a righteous man." Ḥimāiyah then reads the wording of Luke *into* the text from Mark, concluding that the phrase *son of God* merely means *righteous man*. In other words, here the author is not trying to argue that the New Testament is full of contradictions, because he wants to prove that the New Testament itself denies that Christ is the son of God.

(4) *Argumentation*: The author again and again tries to show that the phrase "son of God" is meant merely metaphorically. This phrase was used in the Old Testament already, he states, so why claim that Christ is unique in this regard? The phrase is meant metaphorically in the New Testament as well, according to Ḥimāiyah, and therefore the passages that appear to show only the human nature of Christ must be used to explain those passages that seem to contradict this claim.

(5) *Omission of texts*. Evidently, the author virtually uses only prooftexts from the four gospels, albeit stripped of their contextual environment. He omits almost all the epistles of the New Testament, especially the letters of Paul, but also the letter to the Hebrews and others.

(6) *Omission of topics*. Furthermore, Ḥimāiyah does not address the most important topic according to Christian creeds and doctrine, that is, the crucifixion and resurrection of Christ. The author only very briefly touches on these issues – and the reason for this is doctrinal as well. Only at the end of his tract does the author touch on the issue of the suffering and crucifixion of Christ, as will be shown below.

4.3.2.2. Ḥimāiyah's Doctrinal Approach

It has become clear that the author is being guided in his thinking by some basic assumptions about the definition of God. He understands God in a metaphysical way as being almighty, omniscient, invisible, and impassible. These divine attributes serve as a somewhat axiomatic system which he uses to delegitimize the New Testament accounts. If Christians claim the Christ to be the son of God,

Ḥimāiyah argues, then the attributes of the divine would all necessarily have to be ascribed to him. But doing so would mean that these attributes would exclude various things said about Christ in the four gospels. If Christ really is God, the author emphasizes, it would never be possible for Satan to take Christ to a certain place and speak to him, the way it is reported in the gospels. In the same way, if Christ is said to be God, the author continues, to whom then does he pray when he is crucified – to himself, or to some other God? If Christ is said to be God, and if God is claimed to be invisible, then how can Christ, who is clearly visible, be called God? If Christ admits according to the gospels that he does not know the last day or hour, but God does – how then can Christ be said to be God, since he apparently lacks omniscience?

These few examples suffice to show that Ḥimāiyah measures the testimony of the four gospels according to his understanding of God as a transcendent being, as a God who according to Islamic tradition does not reveal anything about *himself,* but only about *his will*, as a God who is therefore not primarily an object of theological reflection, since learned reflection should rather concentrate on the Qur'an and the Ḥadīth in an attempt to understand God's will. Islamic learning therefore mainly consists of Qur'anic studies and exegesis (*tafsīr* in Arabic), along with all its branches of study, and of the attempt to understand God's will by developing Islamic law (*fiqh* in Arabic), rather than philosophy (*falsafa* in Arabic) or science which approaches the attributes of God in a rather philosophical manner (*kalām* in Arabic).

Even though Ḥimāiyah does not attempt to understand the Christian sources according to *their self-understanding*, he is nevertheless hesitant – up until this point, at any rate – to call all Christian sources "corrupted texts" (*taḥrīf* in Arabic). The reason may be of an apologetical nature, since he wants to convince the reader, whether she be Christian or Muslim, that the texts of the four gospels, rightly understood, contain proofs that Christ is a mere human being, as well as proofs that he is a messenger, as the Islamic tradition makes him out to be. Therefore it seems that the author avoids categorically rejecting the validity of the four gospels, in order to use them as tools for *da'wah*, i.e. the call to Islam.

4.3.2.3. Ḥimāiyah's Hermeneutical Approach

Even though we do not find any explicitly hermeneutical reflections in Ḥimāiyah's book, we would be justified in calling his hermeneutical approach a *hermeneutic of suspicion.* Since the author is deeply convinced that Christian teachings are distorted, he constantly tries to distinguish between those texts of the Biblical scriptures that accord with his Islamic understanding of God and Christ, and those texts that according to his understanding must be regarded as distorted texts. The outcome of this approach is that a number of "approved" texts among the Biblical scriptures are used either to interpret or to refute other texts deemed to have been corrupted. The effect of this procedure is that Ḥimāiyah takes none of the storylines of the four gospels seriously, nor the main ideas of scriptures like the letters of John or the letter to the Hebrews, all of which encompass their own theological centers of gravity. At no point does he demonstrate an awareness of the issue that the Muslim understanding of holy scripture and the Christian understanding of holy scriptures might be very different.

Apparently, the author assigns to the Christian scriptures his own understanding of a text regarded as sent down as a message from God (*tanzīl* in Arabic). The hermeneutical effect of this is that the author's understanding of the Christian textual sources is limited to his Muslim understanding of the divine message as a message that can be ascribed only to one author, God himself, as a message that is regarded as perfectly clear, consistent, and without variations. From this perspective it is impossible to admit that different Christian scriptures like the gospels could have different views about the Christ events. Therefore, if any differences occur, then these differences in the Muslim understanding serve as proof that the texts have been distorted, because according to Muslim understanding, the text can only have one author, that is God, and besides that, only a limited number of receivers, namely the prophets. But their messages have to have one and the same content. If therefore the content of former scriptures contradict the content of later divine messages like those given in the Qur'an, then the former scriptures must be deemed as having been distorted.

Hermeneutically speaking, the author does not attempt to understand the Christian way of dealing with scriptural sources (Biblical texts) which makes it possible to treat differences between texts (albeit rather minor differences) as indicative of the wealth of different perspectives that enables Christians to understand the life, work, suffering, death, and resurrection of Christ in a better and deeper way. Therefore the hermeneutical approach of the author may be labeled not only as a hermeneutic of suspicion, but also as a *hermeneutic of self-affirmation*. The Christian side is not regarded as an entity in its own right; it is merely seen as something that is obviously wrong and therefore in need of correction.

To avoid this kind of approach and to widen the scope, it would have been necessary for Ḥimāiyah to distance himself from the Qur'anic view on Christians, at least to a certain extent. It seems that by adhering to the Qur'anic charge that Jews and Christians distorted their scriptures in many ways, the author cannot *let these scriptures speak to him in their own way*. Such a prospect would call for an attempt to envisage – even if only provisionally – these scriptures as consistent with their own internal logic and therefore coherent, even though from a Muslim perspective, their content as such could not be accepted. Had he attempted this, Ḥimāiyah would have grasped at least a little more of the self-understanding of Christian textual sources and Christian beliefs.

4.3.3. Critical Questions from a Christian Perspective

Some critical questions must be raised. Firstly, the question arises as to whether Ḥimāiyah is acquainted with any Christian theology at all, i.e. with the history of Christian theology, beginning with the doctrinal discussions of the first to the sixth centuries of the Christian tradition, and furthermore with confessional traditions like those of the Orthodox, the Roman Catholics, and the Protestants, not to mention the European theological debates of the 19th and 20th centuries and up until today. There is in Ḥimāiyah's writing not a single reference to any one of the great

Christian theologians such as Augustine, Thomas Aquinas, Luther, Calvin, the authors of the Second Vatican Council, Karl Barth, Karl Rahner, Paul Tillich, Jürgen Moltmann, and so on. And not only does Ḥimāiyah appear to be ignorant of the Christian theological heritage, but he also seems entirely uninformed about Christian exegesis of the Biblical scriptures, particularly of the New Testament. There is not a single reference to Christian exegesis, which means that the author appears to be satisfied with confining himself to his own reading of the New Testament and to his own limited selection of verses.

Ḥimāiyah thus uses the New Testament as little more than a basket of texts from which to cherrypick the very verses he needs to reinforce his own opinion. He himself deems his approach to be quite neutral, as demonstrated by the circumstance that he (at least in the first part of his book) avoids citing verses from the Qur'an as proof of his claims. Since there are a number of Muslim authors who do precisely that, Ḥimāiyah – compared to the others – is indeed more open to debate, although in the course of his book it becomes clear that his only intent is to refute all manner of Christian doctrines.

The author always argues by presuming his own axioms. He does not attempt to follow the line of thought of any of the four gospels, and he never raises the question in what way the Christian idea of an incarnate God could make sense in any way. This way of arguing, i.e. of raising one's own questions and then supplying one's own answers from Biblical verses stripped of their contexts as proof is reminiscent of apologetic activists like the famous Ahmed Deedat from South Africa, who is very popular in many Muslim majority countries to this day. Even though Ḥimāiyah does not quote Ahmed Deedat, his approach is very similar.

Ḥimāiyah's approach is certainly apologetic in its tone, format, and argumentation. We will need to inquire more closely also into the kind of dialogical elements he uses in his attempt to disprove Christian doctrines. We will return to this inquiry below. Before we do so, we should first study his view of the authenticity and originality of Christian doctrine and praxis.

4.4. The Third Line of Argument – The Trinity as Paganism

4.4.1. Thesis: The Trinity Contradicts Human Reason and the Qur'an

Another line of argument Ḥimāiyah pursues is that believing in the Trinity while holding that God is the creator of all conflicts with human reason. Being the creator of all would imply that he created everything that might be called "son," and therefore it is illogical to use the name "son of God" for an entity supposed to be divine. The author concludes that the Trinity stands in conflict with both the Qur'an and human reason. He asks how this could have happened, since in Christian sources, there are prooftexts establishing a proper understanding, such as Matt. 5:17, where Christ says: "Do not think I have come to abolish the Law or the Prophets; I have not come to abolish them but to fulfill them." Ḥimāiyah argues that this verse is proof that Christ understood his own task as that of a messenger sent to confirm the messages of former prophets. Ḥimāiyah then points to the Christian claim that Matt. 28:19, "Therefore go and make disciples of all nations, baptizing them in the name of the Father and of the Son and of the Holy Spirit" serves as proof for a Trinitarian understanding of the New Testament scriptures. He exhorts Christians to avoid this false teaching by searching for verses in the gospels that could confirm the true meaning of these words, which – in his view, at any rate – are and must be congruent with the arguments of the Qur'an and with human reason. In this way, Ḥimāiyah insists on a certain hermeneutical procedure to affirm that the Qur'anic view on Christ is correct. In fact, he himself uses this method in his tract.

4.4.2. Question: Why is the Trinity Not Mentioned in the Gospels?

After arguing that even ordinary Christian laypeople are unable to understand the meaning of the doctrine of Trinity (because, in his view, it is unreasonable anyway), Ḥimāiyah proceeds to reflect on the prerequisites for believing in what a messenger claimed to be the message sent down upon him. Ḥimāiyah raises the question as to why the Trinity is not mentioned in the gospels and other scriptures of the New Testament. The answer he supplies is that something must have gone wrong in the process of transmission. The question remains: What characterizes the contents of a trustworthy prophetic message? What are the hallmarks of proper transmission?

4.4.2.1. Conditions for Proper Transmission

Ḥimāiyah argues (1) that the content of a proper message must be uttered *frequently*: Since the message always remains the same, it must corroborate the messages of prophets in earlier times. Furthermore, (2) since every prophet spoke the language of his own people, the different messages have to be translated and compared by a translator able to speak both languages perfectly to ensure *a proper translation* and to avoid any deviation or alteration. In addition, (3) one has to confirm to the greatest extent possible that *the meaning of the words* to be translated *is congruent with the will of the prophet* who uttered them. This is necessary to avoid the distortion or misinterpretation of the meaning of the words along the chain of messengers.

4.4.2.2. Has the Message of Christ Been Transmitted Accurately?

Having defined the requirements for proper transmission, Ḥimāiyah then applies them to the texts of the Bible, which he evaluates according to the standards of *frequency*, *proper translation*, and, finally, *congruency* with the meaning intended by the earlier messengers and prophets.

Frequency: Ḥimāiyah concludes that nothing in the books of earlier prophets warrants the Christian understanding of God as Father, Son, and Holy Spirit, nor are there any hints to something like a Trinity. He contends: "This text destroys the doctrine of Trinity and explains the servanthood of Christ and denies his divinity."[29] That is to say that the standard of frequency of utterance is not met by the books of earlier prophets.

Proper translation: Next, Ḥimāiyah claims that the "corruption of the Christian doctrine" (*taḥrīf* in Arabic) is due to the fact that there is "a multitude of languages of the gospels," but he does not explain what he means by this. The four gospels of the New Testament are all written in Koiné Greek, and therefore the author's claim does not hold true for these texts. The author provides no indication that he might be referring to the apocryphal gospels. The examples the author provides refer to Hebrew, Aramaic, and Arabic words. Ḥimāiyah refers to John 17:3 to argue that if Christians would adhere to the meaning of these words, they would have to confess pure monotheism. He reasons that if the Trinitarian faith were correct, then – according to this gospel, at any rate – Christ would have had to mention the Trinity at this point.

Again, Ḥimāiyah maintains that John 1:18 and 1 Tim. 6:16 speak of God as being invisible, whereas Christians claim to have seen Christ and the Holy Spirit, and that this is a manifest contradiction since, if the latter truly were God, they would have to be invisible. Ḥimāiyah's arguments turn out to be quite repetitive at times. Besides the question of divine invisibility, the author again brings up the question of divine omniscience which – in his view – Christ claimed not to have (with reference to Mark 13:32), and therefore he cannot be spoken of as being divine in nature. Furthermore, pointing to the first commandment, Ḥimāiyah argues that it would have been incumbent upon Christ to mention the Trinity and not speak of pure monotheism, as he did in Mark 12:29-34. The author references a number of verses (Deut. 4:39, 6:4; Isa. 44:6; and 1 Cor. 8:4-6) to prove his point, contending that these texts all point to pure monotheism and not to a Trinitarian understanding of God.

Congruency: Concerning different words of Christ, Ḥimāiyah quotes Matt. 19:16-17, "Just then a man came up to Jesus and asked: 'Teacher, what good thing must I do to get eternal life?' 'Why do you ask me about what is good?' Jesus replied. 'There is only One who is good.'" This passage Ḥimāiyah takes to mean that Christ himself did not want to be called "good" because only the one God may be called "good." From this, he concludes that if the Trinity were correct, then Jesus would surely have mentioned it at this point.

This counts as an example of the author inquiring into the *will* of a prophet in conveying a certain message. The will of Christ in this instance would be to confirm true monotheism, meaning that the Christian interpretation of his words, which are attested in the Christian sources (in the first three gospels respectively), would amount to a distortion or corruption.

[29] Ḥimāiyah, *Taṯlīṯ*, 74.

4.4.3. Answer: A Corrupted Transmission Process and a False Doctrine

According to Ḥimāiyah, contemporary Christian texts and current Christian doctrine were marred by a less than accurate process of transmission. The Christian message therefore must be regarded as distorted, though not in its entirety. Thus Ḥimāiyah answers his own question in the affirmative, arguing that the Christian religion as it exists today is deeply corrupted. He then proceeds to give examples to warrant the falseness of the Christian doctrine of Trinity.

One of his most important arguments against the Trinity is drawn from Matt. 27:46, 50, "About three in the afternoon Jesus cried out in a loud voice '*Eli, Eli, lema sabachtani?*' (which means 'My God, my God, why have you forsaken me?'). ... And when Jesus had cried out again in a loud voice, he gave up his spirit." Ḥimāiyah argues that

> this saying invalidates the doctrine of the Trinity and destroys it root and branch. For if Christ were God, he would not seek refuge in another God, saying: "My God, my God, why have you forsaken me?" Especially since there are texts in the Old Testament that show that the true and eternal God will not weaken, tire, nor fail.[30]

In support of his argument, Ḥimāiyah appeals to Isa. 40:28, 44:6; Jer. 10:10; Hab. 1:12; and 1 Tim. 1:17.[31]

He also repeats examples he had used before, for example: Jesus as God would not have called himself "Son of man," or: according the Gospel of John he could not have claimed that God is greater than himself. To Ḥimāiyah, the account of the suffering of Jesus in Matt. 26:34-44 is striking evidence against the doctrine of Trinity, since this account denies the divinity of Christ.

4.4.4. Conclusion: The Christian Religion Is a Distorted, Corrupted Doctrine and Praxis

In an emphatic gesture, Ḥimāiyah concludes with rhetorical questions: "Yes! Is it possible for a god to grieve and be depressed?! Is it possible for a god to die while praying to another god?! And if the Christ came into the world to save humankind by his blood, then why all this despair, this depression, and this praying to God for this cup to be taken away?!"[32]

---

[30] Ḥimāiyah, *Taṯlīṯ*, 73.

[31] It is interesting to note that in this section, Ḥimāiyah makes use of al-Kairānawī's book *iẓhār al-ḥaqq*, Part 3, pages 207-208, giving exactly the same Biblical references as al-Kairānawī does, yet not documenting that he is referring to *Izhar al-haqq*. See Maulana Rahmatullah Kairanvi, *Izhar' ul-Haqq: The Truth Revealed*, parts 1-4 (London: Ta Ha Publishers, 1989/90).

[32] Ḥimāiyah, *Taṯlīṯ*, 74-75.

Moving on, Ḥimāiyah levels a number of accusations against the Christian religion in its current state, comparing it with the religion of Christ, the messenger, at the time of his coming:

> The Christian religion was built on the basis of pure and reasonable monotheism, but they turned it into a religion of idolatry by establishing an unreasonable Trinity, taken from the Trinity of the Greeks and the Romans, quoted from the Trinity of the Egyptians and Brahmins in a distorted quote. Taking a religion of heavenly law, they recreated its entire law by abolishing it and replacing it with innovations (arab. *bida*ᶜ) and traditions alien to it. A religion of ascetism, modesty, austerity, altruism, and servanthood (arab. *ᶜabūdīya*), and they turned it into a religion of greed and desire, luxury, selfish-ness and enslavement of human beings.[33]

It is interesting to note that the author increases the number of accusations far beyond what he had been speaking of so far. He lists a number of critical points like greed, pride, luxury, and enslavement, but does not explain what these are supposed to mean. Quoting Rashid Riḍā again, the author proceeds to accuse Paul of having invented a new kind of religion.

4.5. Ḥimāiyah's Sources

Even though Ḥimāiyah uses only very few sources, it is important to note the context of those he does use. Among the authors he cites, at least two deserve closer consideration. The first is *Ibn Ḥazm* (d. 1064), the second *Raḥmatullāh Khalīl al-'Uthmānī al-Kairānawī* (1818-1891). These authors feature prominently in the debate about the Islamic charge that Jewish and Christian scriptures were corrupted. We now have to turn to these authors in order to understand the significance of their charges within the broader Islamic discussion of these issues.

4.5.1. The Charge of Interpretative or Textual Distortion of the Scriptures (taḥrīf)

According to Camilla Adang, "Islamic polemics against Judaism and its adherents is a phenomenon as old as Islam itself, and the Qur'an is its first source."[34] Let us proceed by briefly considering some prominent examples of Muslim authors engaging in Islamic polemics.

---

[33] Ḥimāiyah, *Taṯlīṯ*, 75.

[34] Camilla Adang, "Medieval Muslim Polemics against the Jewish Scripture," in Jean Jacques Waardenburg, ed., *Muslim Perceptions of Other Religions: A Historical Survey* (Oxford: Oxford University Press, 1999), 143.

4.5.2. Sources

4.5.2.1. Abū Muḥammad 'Alī Ibn Aḥmad Ibn Ḥazm aẓ-Ẓāhirī al-Andalusī (994-1064)

The medieval author Ibn Ḥazm grew up in Al-Andalus in the 11th century. He wrote a number of books to refute the truth claims of Jews and Christians, such as the *Exposition of the Alterations That Jews and Christians Have Effected in the Torah and the Gospel* (*Izhār Tabdīl al-Yahūd wa'l-Naṣārā li'l-Tawrāt wa'l Injīl* in Arabic). His main argument is that the Jewish Torah could not be used by Muslims, neither as a legal source, nor as an historical one. He attempts to prove this argument with reference to the Pentateuch by alleging that these books are full of errors, contradictions, and inconsistencies. Ibn Ḥazm also argues from an historical perspective that the actual text Moses had received on Mount Sinai was lost in antiquity. In addition, Ibn Ḥazm declares more than 20 Jewish kings after David and Solomon to have been idol worshippers, claiming that only one copy of the text given to Moses had been left in the temple, and that this text had been altered by the high priests, the only ones with access to the text. But when Jerusalem was conquered by Nebuchadnezzar, the temple was destroyed and the text of Moses along with it. Hundreds of years later, he alleges, the Jews rewrote the Torah.

Ibn Ḥazm concludes that the text of the Pentateuch has been corrupted in many ways. Adang summarizes Ibn Ḥazm's approach:

> Both analyses lead [Ibn Ḥazm] to conclude that the Torah as it was known in his days was not to be equated with the text originally revealed to Moses, which must now be presumed lost. ... According to Ibn Ḥazm, Ezra directed a new Torah, allegedly from his memory but in reality changing it so dramatically that the result no longer resembles the divine original. It is on this false 'revelation' that the Jewish religion is based.[35]

Therefore, Ibn Ḥazm contends, the distorted Jewish scriptures (the Torah) must be seen for what they are: a textual alteration.

Theodore Pulcini summarizes some arguments of Ibn Ḥazm according to Ibn Ḥazm´s *Treatise on Obvious Contradictions and Evident Lies* (arab. *Faṣl fī munaqāḍāt ẓāhira wa-takādhīb wāḍiha*). The similarity between Himaiyah, writing in the 21st century, and Ibn Ḥazm, who lived 11th century, is striking. Pulcini on the arguments of Ibn Ḥazm:

> „Furthermore, the New Testament compromises the transcendence of God. In it Jesus clearly describes himself as eating and drinking (cf. Mt. 11:18). If he were God, this would mean that God eats and drinks! This is inconsistent with God´s total otherness. And the Christians cannot say in response that only his humanity ate while his

[35] Adang, *Medieval Muslim Polemics*, 152f.

> divinity did not, even they admit that Christ´s humanity and divinity were always united. It therefore cannot be said that only 'half´ of Christ ate and drank. [2:32]. The New Testament also compromises divine omniscience in that it attributes factually incorrect statements to Christ. For example, in Matthew´s gospel Christ is depicted as describing the mustard tree as supporting a number of birds and their nests (Mt. 13:31-32). This is absurd, Ibn Ḥazm argues; the mustard plant could not support upon itself a single bird. No prophet could say such a thing, let alone God [2:34]! The New Testament denies omnipotence and majesty. The gospel of Matthew, for instance, maintains that Christ could not perform many miracles in his home country (13:58). If Christ were God, how could this be so? Lack of power to perform miracles is not a proper attribute of God; after all, the Qur´ān clearly states that miracles come from God (6:109) [2:35-36] Ibn Ḥazm also points to the passages in which Jesus is depicted as praying in anguish in the Garden of Gethsemane (cf. Mt. 26:39ff., Mk. 14:35ff., Lk. 22:41ff.) and crying out in agony on the cross (>My God, my God, why hast thou forsaken me?< cf. Mt. 27:46, Mk. 15:34). Are such scenes appropriate to God? Must God be consoled by angels? Must he ask to be delivered from death? Would he sweat in anguish over his impending death? Can he, as God, be abandoned by God? All of this is nonsense."[36]

Other Muslim authors took a more cautious approach, arguing that the alteration took place only as a matter of *interpretation*. The author of the first commentary to the Qur'an, for instance, Muqātil ibn Sulaymān (d. 767), commenting on the *taḥrīf*-verses of the Qur'an, tells a number of stories to explain that it was not the text of the Jewish scriptures itself that was corrupted, but only the Jewish interpretation of them, since the Jews denied the prophethood of Muḥammad and did not acknowledge the very passages of their own scriptures that – according to Muqātil ibn Sulaymān – foretell the coming the prophet Muḥammad.[37]

During the Middle Ages, a number of Muslim authors claimed the scriptures of Jews and Christians to have been corrupted either by a kind of *textual distortion* or a kind of *interpretative corruption* or a combination of both. But during the 19th century, things once again changed dramatically.[38]

---

[36] Theodore Pulcini, Exegesis as Polemical Discourse: Ibn Ḥazm on Jewish and Christian Scriptures. Atlanta: Scholars Press, 1998, 109.

[37] Gordon D. Nickel, "Early Muslim Accusations of Taḥrīf: Muqātil ibn Sulaymān's Commentary on Key Qur'anic Verses," in David Thomas, ed., *The Bible in Arab Christianity* (Leiden: Brill, 2007), 207 ff.

[38] Mun'im Sirry, Scriptural Polemics. The Qur'ān and Other Religions, Oxford: Oxford University Press, 2014, 110-132.

4.5.2.2. Raḥmatullāh ibn Khalīl al-'Uthmānī al-Kairānawī al-Hindī (1818-1891)

By the middle of the 19th century, the results of European Biblical scholarship became known in the Muslim world. The application of the historical-critical method led European philologists to the conclusion that the Biblical texts were not trustworthy. Apologists like the Indian Shia scholar Raḥmatullāh Khalīl al-'Uthmānī al-Kairānawī (1818-1891) therefore argued that after applying scholarly methods, even the Christians were now convinced that the Islamic charge concerning the distortion of the scriptures of Jews and Christians was true. In his book *Exposition of the Truth* (*iẓhār al-ḥaqq* in Arabic), al-Kairānawī makes extensive use of the results of historical-critical and liberal theology of European origin. He had received these insights from his coworker, Dr. Muḥammad Wazīr Khān, a doctor who had spent some years in Great Britain, during which he gathered a significant amount of historical-critical material.[39] Schirrmacher states concerning the *iẓhār al-ḥaqq*:

> Only a few polemical Muslim works have become as famous as al-Kairānawī's *iẓhār al-ḥaqq*. It has been stated: "The first great classic of modern Muslim polemic has never been superseded." ... Undoubtedly, the book played a key role for Muslim polemics in the past, but it is still currently on the "top ten" of Muslim apologetical works.[40]

The book was translated into different languages and has been republished many times ever since. The influence of the book has therefore been widespread. What was new in al-Kairānawī's approach was the fact that he referred to liberal theological works by European scholars:

> Al-Kairānawī was – ostensibly – the very first apologist in the Muslim world who referred to these books and Bible commentaries in order to fight Christianity with its own weapons. For the first time, he used different works of famous European theologians who were influenced by liberalism and historical criticism of European theology of the nineteenth century.[41]

Schirrmacher rightly concludes:

> Here it is obvious that al-Kairānawī has changed the former Muslim view of taḥrīf and the Muslim view of Christianity as a whole. ... Apologists in former times only criticized certain Biblical dogmas such as Trinity or the dogma of the deity of Jesus Christ as

[39] Christine Schirrmacher, "The Influence of Higher Bible Criticism on Muslim Apologetics in the Nineteenth Century," in Jean Jacques Waardenburg, ed., *Muslim Perceptions of Other Religions: A Historical Survey* (Oxford: Oxford University Press, 1999), 270-279.

[40] Schirrmacher, *Influence of Higher Bible Criticism*, 272-273.

[41] Schirrmacher, *Influence of Higher Bible Criticism*, 273.

> the Qur'an does. Al-Kairānawī expanded the Qur'anic criticism of the corruption of the Bible to a much larger extent. Leading Muslim apologists now follow the example of *iẓhār al-ḥaqq* and take over the "results" of the textual studies of European theologians. Al-Kairānawī came to the conclusion that the Biblical texts are totally distorted, corrupted, and unreliable in all their historical, dogmatical, and narrative passages.[42]

The 1989/1990 reprint edition of *Iẓhār al-ḥaqq*, published by the London based Ta-Ha Publications, comprises approximately 500 pages. The first part is entitled *The Books of the Bible*, the second part is devoted to the topic of *Contradictions and Errors in the Biblical text*, the third and longest part (running to more than 200 pages) is entitled *Distortion and Abrogation in the Bible: The Trinity Refused*, and the fourth part is entitled *Proof of the Divine Origin of the Qur'an and the Authority of the Ḥadīths*.[43] The biggest part of *Iẓhār al-ḥaqq* deals with alleged distortions of Biblical texts, which al-Kairānawī seeks to prove by quoting a number of European authors from the first half of the 19th century. Even in his attempts to refute the doctrine of the Trinity, the question of distorted texts remains dominant. At the end of the third part, al-Kairānawī gives some explanations as to why the doctrine of the Trinity must be false, appealing to divine attributes like invisibility or indivisibility to show that Christ could not be called God or son of God. These considerations are based on a metaphysical thinking in categories of substances.

4.5.2.3. Rashīd Riḍā (1865-1935)

Of great importance was the fact that both ordinary Muslim laypeople and Muslim scholars like the famous Rashīd Riḍā made use of the book. Schirrmacher states:

> The influence of *iẓhār al-ḥaqq* can be noted in the nineteenth century "reform-wing" Sunni theologian Rashīd Riḍā's extensive use of the work when dealing with Christianity. Coming to the question of Muḥammad's mission, he quoted in the famous Abduh / Riḍā Qur'an commentary *tafsīr al-qur'ān al-ḥakīm* about 60 pages from *iẓhār al-ḥaqq*. Another Muslim polemicist who used *iẓhār al-ḥaqq* is Muḥammad Abū Zahra. In his "Lectures on Christianity" (*muḥāḍarāt fī an-naṣrānīya*) he referred to al-Kairānawī's commentaries on the Christian creed.[44]

Seeing as the work of Rashīd Riḍā continues to enjoy prominence among Muslim scholars worldwide today, we should proceed by providing some information

[42] Schirrmacher, *Influence of Higher Bible Criticism*, 275.

[43] Kairanvi, *Izhar-Ul-Haqq*.

[44] Schirrmacher, *Influence of Higher Bible Criticism*, 273.

about his life and work. Born in Syria, Riḍā later became a student of the famous Egyptian reformer, scholar, and mufti Muḥammad 'Abduh.[45] In 1911/1912, Riḍā founded the first Islamic seminary for *da'wah*, the propagation of Islam. In 1905, he began working together with Muḥammad 'Abduh on a commentary to the Qur'an called *al-Manar*. Riḍā's work aimed at creating a purified and explicitly modern form of Islam by way of a return to the roots of Islamic identity as given in the heritage of the prophet and his companions, the rightly-guided forefathers (*as-salaf as-salih* in Arabic). Against the backdrop of traditional learning, Riḍā proposed a new style of Islamic teaching. In addition to the study of the Qur'an, the Arabic language, its grammar, and so forth, he called for the study of new topics like sociology, politology, geography, and the English language in order to respond to the challenges of modernity. Riḍā was deeply convinced that the technological achievements of the West actually derived from Islamic philosophy and tradition, with the West simply developing and building on Islamic ideas. With Islam purified according to the standards of the rightly-guided forefathers, Riḍā argued that the Islamic world could once again become the champion of human civilization it had been in former times.

Riḍā took a critical stance towards Christianity, accusing the church of having corrupted Western civilization by teaching people to follow myths and believe in miracles, and by making people depend on irrational beliefs and on the authority of priests and monks. Riḍā attempted to develop Muslim mission as a countermeasure against Christian mission societies, and so he was also interested in refuting Christian doctrine and Christian truth claims in general. He therefore devoted long passages in his works to a polemical apologetic approach, arguing against Christian teachings. In doing so, he relied – as mentioned above – on the writings of such authors as al-Kairānawī.

It is remarkable how often Ḥimāiyah quotes works of Rashid Riḍā. In his tract on the Trinity, he cites Riḍā no less than nine times (out of a total of 113 references). He refers to al-Kairānawī's *Iẓhār al-ḥaqq* ten times, to Ahmed Deedat's books eleven times, to Abū Zahra once, and to Sayyid Qutb twice.

4.5.2.4. Ahmed Deedat (1918-2005)

Wherever you travel around the world, you are liable to find in mosques and Muslim bookstores any number of video-tapes, audio-cassettes, and books by Ahmed Deedat. Deedat is seen by many Muslims as the most famous anti-Christian preacher of our time. Phillip Scheepers rightly points out:

> It is probably fair to say that Sheikh Ahmed Hussein Deedat (1918-2005) does not enjoy high levels of name recognition in Western Christian circles. Yet this South African born Muslim apologist is regarded by many within the Muslim world as one of the greatest

[45] E.E. Shahin, *The Oxford Encyclopedia of the Modern Islamic World*, vol. 3 (Oxford: Oxford University Press, 1995), s.v. "Rashid Riḍā, Muḥammad."; Yvonne Haddad, "Muhammad Abduh: Pioneer of Islamic Reform," in Ali Rahnema, ed., *Pioneers of Islamic Revival* (London: Atlantic Highlands, 1994), 30-63.

> ever Islamic scholars of the Bible. This is evidenced by the string of awards that he has received from governments all around the Muslim world (including the prestigious "King Faisal Prize for Service to Islam" awarded by the king of Saudi Arabia in 1986). One of the main reasons behind Deedat's fame was the fact that he claimed to radically undermine the Christian faith by referencing the key texts of Christianity itself. This approach was markedly different from standard Muslim responses to Christianity that tended to simply reference Qur'anic teaching that Christianity was superseded by Islam (cf. Qur'an 17:89) and leave it at that. He was also a masterful debater and had superb command of the English language.[46]

Born in 1918 in India (in what is today the Gujarat province), Deedat left India for South Africa in 1927. After leaving school, Deedat worked as a shopkeeper in Durban. Since the shop was located near to a Christian seminary, he came into contact with students. After theological debates with these students, Deedat sometimes felt insulted and unable to respond properly. Therefore he devoted more and more time to studying the Qur'an. When he came to read al-Kairānawī's *Iẓhār al-ḥaqq*, he began to call people to Allah, using Biblical texts to show that the Christian teachings are distorted and that the message of the Qur'an is the ultimate truth. In 1958, he started the *Islamic Propagation Center* in the city of Durban. In the following years, he held many lectures on Christianity and Islam and took part in some famous debates, including one in 1986 with the well-known televangelist Jimmy Swaggart.[47]

Scheepers notes:

> Despite his worldwide success life was not all plain sailing for Deedat. Many Muslims felt deeply uncomfortable with his aggressive approach, claiming (with some justice) that it alienated the very constituency he was supposedly trying to reach. Others questioned aspects of his theology with some Muslim leaders going as far as claiming that his positions deviated from orthodox Muslim teaching. Such claims led to several protracted pamphlet wars between Deedat and other Muslim leaders.[48]

The book *The Choice* gives a good impression of Deedat's way of arguing. It is a combination of storytelling and the citation of verses from the Bible and the Qur'an.[49] We will provide an example in the next section.

---

[46] Phillip Scheepers, "An Analysis of the Christology of Sheikh Ahmed Deedat," *Vox Reformata* 2016: 1.

[47] Scheepers, *Deedat*, 5.

[48] Scheepers, *Deedat*, 5.

[49] Ahmed Deedat, *The Choice: Islam and Christianity*, Vol. 1 (Doha: Fahil Khair, 1994).

4.5.3. Comparing Ḥimāiyah to Former Apologists

After analyzing Ḥimāiyah's book on the Trinity, we found that he refers to a number of Muslim scholars who could be called apologetic. Nevertheless, these authors clearly differ in their approach. Al-Kairānawī, for instance, attempts to make use of European books on Biblical criticism to show that the Biblical scriptures have been distorted. His argumentation concentrates on different readings of texts according to different textual manuscripts, on apocryphal literature, and so forth. In dealing with Christian teachings, al-Kairānawī picks out particular verses like Mark 13:32, claiming that the doctrine of Trinity must be false because Christ admits not knowing when the day of judgement will come. Al-Kairānawī therefore states:

> Christ clearly precludes both himself and others from this knowledge, and he does so without any reservations. Had Christ been one of the hypostatic persons of God, this absence of knowledge of the Day of Judgement would not have been conceivable for him, especially when keeping in view the belief that the Word and the Son together are the "knowledge of God," and that the Word, the Son, and Christ are united together in one being.[50]

Ahmed Deedat takes a different approach. He devotes long passages to what he regards as the exegesis of Biblical verses. For instance, he cites Deut. 18:18, arguing that the words "I will raise up for them a prophet like you from among their fellow Israelites, and I will put my words in his mouth. He will tell them everything I command him" do not refer to Jesus, but must be understood as a prediction of the prophet Muḥammad.[51] In a passage that is fifteen pages long, Deedat accumulates a number of arguments to underscore that this prophecy cannot refer to Jesus, but must be a reference to Muḥammad. He focuses on the words "like you," arguing that there are a number of similarities between Moses and Muḥammad, whereas Jesus is different. Both Moses and Muḥammad had a father and a mother, and both had a natural birth, whereas Jesus did not (Surah 3:47). Both Moses and Muḥammad were married, were accepted by their people, introduced new laws and regulations, and died naturally, whereas Christ did not. Therefore, Deedat concludes, the Christian claim that Deut. 18:18 refers to Jesus is false and the Muslim claim that this verse prophesies the coming of Muḥammad is correct.

This example highlights a general tendency in the writing of Deedat. His underlying concern is to show that the Muslim understanding of Christ is true, rather than to prove that the Biblical scriptures are distorted, even though this remains the unquestioned basis of all his assumptions and claims. Like al-Kairānawī, Deedat also does not interpret Biblical references within their own context and does not attempt to comprehend Christian teachings according to the Christian self-understanding. This can be shown by quoting from a passage on the Trinity. Deedat cites John 14:23 and then goes on to say in a folksy manner:

[50] Kairanvi, *Izhar ul Haqq*, vol. 3, 206.

[51] Deedat, *Choice*, 6-21.

> Please don't worry. You are not really expected to understand the above verbiage. In short the Christian believes that the "THREE" (I beg your pardon, the Christian says, "ONE!"), all the *three* are supposed to be Omnipresent and Omniscient and as such lead us to an amusing and ridiculous conclusion. Jesus (p[eace] b[e] u[pon] h[im]) according to the Christians agonized on the cross at Calvary. Being "*inseparable*," the Father and the Holy Ghost also must have agonized with the Son, and when he died, the other two died with him! Little wonder we hear the cry in the West – "*God is Dead!*" Don't laugh. All this imposes on us a more sombre responsibility of extricating our Christian brethren from the spiritual quagmire into which they are wallowing.[52]

The quotation shows the insulting manner in which Deedat treats Christian sources like the Gospel of John. The text of the gospel is called "verbiage," which is a derogatory term indicating that it must be a distorted text. Deedat's conclusion – if Christ dies, the Father and the Holy Spirit die with him – shows that he is not willing to accept the Christian understanding that speaking of God means speaking about the relations of God, the Father, Christ Jesus, the Son, and the Holy Spirit. We will need to return to this observation later on.

Compared with al-Kairānawī and Deedat, Ḥimāiyah's deliberations are less insulting, even though he from time to time addresses Christians directly. Ḥimāiyah is not concerned with lengthy recapitulations of historical criticism, as is al-Kairānawī, nor does he engage in an ongoing process of refuting Christian doctrines in a folksy manner, as Deedat does. Ḥimāiyah aims at a somewhat more scholarly approach, as he sees it. Even though he at times borrows arguments from other authors, he first tries to refute Christian doctrines by using mainly Christian sources. Nevertheless, the result is almost identical to that of the two others, since he also charges that Christians have distorted the true religion of the Christ by adopting pagan religious ideas, such as the Trinity. – The question then remains: In what sense – if at all – may Ḥimāiyah's approach be called dialogical? Is Ḥimāiyah actually "in dialogue" with Christian source texts and authors? And if so, what kind of a "dialogue" is this?

4.6. In What Sense May Ḥimāiyah's Approach Be Called Dialogical?

4.6.1. Dialogue – Kinds and Levels of Dialogue

The word "dialogue" means two persons speaking with each other by raising arguments and counterarguments. Both parties reason with each other. Even so, there are different understandings about the aim of such dialogue. What does one or the other party, or what do both parties believe the aim of such mutual reasoning to

[52] Deedat, *Choice*, 83.

be? Is there a shared understanding of the purpose of the dialogue? It would seem necessary to proceed by clarifying different levels and kinds of dialogue, before turning to the specific goals people may have in engaging in dialogue.

4.6.1.1. Contact Dialogue

We may follow *Henning Wrogemann* in distinguishing between different levels and kinds of dialogue. He differentiates between contact dialogues, information dialogues, consensus dialogues, and persuasion dialogues. Each form of dialogue shows a specific kind of reciprocity; each form of dialogue has its own "environment." Contact dialogues usually take place on an official political level; information dialogues usually take place on social and academic levels; consensus dialogue usually takes place on local grassroots levels and also on the political level; and persuasion dialogues often take place in an informal manner in everyday life or on special occasions such as lectures or interreligious debates. Let us begin with contact dialogue. What is a contact dialogue? Wrogemann explains:

> By *contact dialogue* we mean different collective we's meeting at regular intervals. In the Bosnian war, for instance, delegations from the warring parties, i.e., of Croats, Bosnians, and Serbs, would regularly meet. Usually they did not meet to discuss any particular points or for any specific purposes. Rather, the point was that they met. It was the get-together itself that was significant there. Another example is the words of greeting customarily spoken in many countries, where a representative from one religious configuration will bring greetings at significant festivals of another religion. For example, in Egypt, the Coptic pope might speak words of greeting at the Islamic Feast of the Sacrifice, just as a Muslim dignitary might congratulate Christians at Christmas. These instances, too, are not about the content as such but rather about the symbolism of being invited and bringing greetings. The significance of such gestures should not be underestimated, especially in conflict-laden societal situations. This is about risky acts of mutual recognition in lifeworldly contexts in the sense of a theory of gift giving.[53]

Evidently, none of the authors mentioned above in our study is concerned with contact dialogues of this kind. Instead, their writings might be classified as an information dialogue instead, since the authors use both Muslim and Christian sources. Therefore, one might assume that the intention is to provide better information than is commonly available. Is this the case?

4.6.1.2. Information Dialogue

What are the features of an information dialogue? Wrogemann states:

[53] Henning Wrogemann, *A Theology of Interreligious Relations*, trans. Karl E. Böhmer (Downers Grove, IL: IVP Academic, 2019), 308.

> Compared to the mostly symbolic communication of contact dialogues, information dialogues are a type of dialogue where verbal exchanges play a fundamental role. In Germany, for example, many Christian-Muslim encounters initiated between church congregations and mosque congregations may be labeled as information dialogues. The point is to gain firsthand knowledge about the lifestyle, practices, doctrines, values, and day-to-day life of the religious Other. The specific *intention* consists, first, of getting to know more about the Others and of being exposed to certain shared experiences. In other words, the intent is to bring about an *increase of information*. The idea is for this increase—and this is the second intention—to contribute toward *overcoming prejudices* and to make it possible to see the respective Others in a new light.

The form of *reciprocity* unique to this type consists, first, *in entrusting oneself to the self portrayed by the respective Other*, that is, of not assuming that the Other is out to trick you, that he is ignorant, or that he is misinformed. Second, reciprocity ideally consists in the willingness t*o call one's own prejudices into question and to allow others to call them into question as well.* As it is, this presupposes not only a modicum of trust but also a certain degree of equanimity in order to embrace the possibility of attendant insecurities— after all, the sense of orientation afforded by prior convictions is temporarily suspended. A third form of reciprocity consists in being prepared genuinely to examine the information proffered by the Other, which includes being open to accept new interpretations that might possibly arise from this examination.[54]

In the writings of Ḥimāiyah and others, we have found no signs of the authoris calling their own position and point of view into question. They are not concerned with clarifying prejudices, and they show no intention to set aside their own truth claims even for a second. Therefore the label of information dialogue would seem to be inapplicable to their approaches.

4.6.1.3. Consensus Dialogue

Even less is it possible to ascribe the label of consensus dialogue to these approaches. The features of consensus dialogues, according to Wrogemann, are as follows:

> In consensus dialogues, participants examine the traditions, teachings, and practices of the respective Others with a view to determining whether their own preconceptions accurately reflect the profile of the religious Others. Not only that, but they also examine them in order to determine whether they are true in the full sense of the word. This means that ideally, the reciprocal learning refers not only to the correct representation of the issues at stake, but—above and beyond that—also to the *religious learning potential*. It is assumed

[54] Wrogemann, *A Theology of Interreligious Relations*, 309.

> that potentially, the familiar truth from one's own tradition and experience is to a greater or lesser extent also present in other traditions, or, alternatively, that religious traditions participate in a transcendent reality that is also definitive for one's own tradition.[55]

Ḥimāiyah and other authors are not open to any reciprocal kind of learning, since they clearly presuppose that the Qur'an provides the ultimate truths. In their minds, therefore, the other side representing the Christian perspective needs to be corrected, and nothing is to be learned from the other side except what has already been revealed by the Qur'an. The authors fully intend to persuade Christians and Jews that they should follow the recommendations of the Qur'an to embrace Islam and follow the prophet Muḥammad.

4.6.1.4. Persuasion Dialogue

What are the features of a persuasion dialogue? Wrogemann explains:

> In persuasion dialogues, participants assume the possibility of genuine interreligious learning in the sense of specific religious experiences. However, whereas in the consensus dialogue type, the direction of the learning potential cannot be defined ahead of time, for the reason that this kind of learning is possible *in all directions*, in the case of the persuasion dialogue type, every participant presupposes such a direction. For example, A would assume that if only B assessed A's arguments as impartially as possible, in all likelihood, after a certain amount of time, B would be convinced by A's arguments, thereby adopting A's position. B would then convert to the religion or worldview of A. This type of dialogue frequently occurs in day-to-day conversations, but it is also found in things such as apologetic literature. The basic assumption is that because the truth represented by one's own claim to religious ultimate validity is the ultimate truth, all people will find it convincing. Frequently, people interpret this truth as being intrinsic to the world, and for this reason they assume that all people (possibly even all creatures) will evince a quasi-natural disposition to embrace this truth. The persuasive force of the dialogue is therefore ascribed not so much to the rhetorical skill of a human dialogue participant or her ability to persuade the Other by way of logic, but rather to the persuasiveness inherent to this ultimate truth.[56]

This description certainly fits the type of dialogue Ḥimāiyah engages in, as mentioned in the introduction of his book. As cited above, he writes:

---

[55] Wrogemann, *A Theology of Interreligious Relations*, 310.

[56] Wrogemann, *A Theology of Interreligious Relations*, 311.

> This is the seventh book in a series on the field of comparative religion that I present to the reader in an easy way. I order the evidence and the arguments and proceed by way of scholarly investigation, drawing on the most correct and documented sources. Our book deals with the doctrine of Trinity on the basis of Christian sources and holy books. I try to present them carefully and honestly, without going beyond them or misrepresenting their beliefs. The earnest reader will find in this research the evidence and proofs that illuminate the way for him to know the truth and to attain it. I do not want to write a conclusion on the content of this book in this introduction. ... It is better to let the reader himself discover the truth, in order to enable him to exercise by himself the right to accept or reject it. And Allah guides whom he wills to a straight path.[57]

According to this passage, Ḥimāiyah expects careful readers to come to their own conclusions, by which he means that they will ultimately embrace Islam because of the rational proof provided, which human reason cannot but accept. This kind of dialogue may be called *da'wah*-dialogue, since it is aimed at convincing people of the truth revealed in the Qur'an. What are the features of this kind of dialogue, as seen in the book of Ḥimāiyah?

4.6.2. Ḥimāiyah's Hermeneutic of a Da'wah-dialogue

4.6.2.1. Persuasion by Human Reason and Simplicity of Thought

Ḥimāiyah's approach rests on the assumption that religious teachings must accord with human reasoning. Therefore, he attempts to depict the Muslim understanding of the one God and his revelation as *reasonable*. Like many other authors engaged in the call to Islam (*da'wah* in Arabic), Ḥimāiyah argues that the teachings of Islam are actually simple and easy to grasp. He contrasts this simplicity with the complexity of Christian teachings, and compares the rationality of Islam with the alleged irrationality of Christian creeds and dogma. His hypothesis is that if people (and Christians especially) would only use their rational capacities in an ordinary manner, they would *necessarily* come to the conclusion that Islam is right (and that Christianity is wrong). Therefore, all that Ḥimāiyah needs to do is to convey these arguments in a simple manner; there is no need to emphasize the arguments or to insult the Other (even though some of Ḥimāiyah's remarks of could be understood as insulting.)

4.6.2.2. Principles of Truth Are Seen as Timeless and Congruent

According to the Qur'anic understanding of the prophets, it is held that "we make no difference between them," meaning that all of the prophets are regarded as conveying the same message. Though they may do so in different times and places, the message nevertheless remains the same. The reason for this is that according to

[57] Ḥimāiyah, *Taṯlīṯ*, Preface (no numbering).

the Muslim understanding, there is only *one author* of the divine message, namely the one and only God himself, who by the process of transmission via the angel Gabriel ensures that the message does not become distorted. This means that truth is actually timeless, that it remains one and the same, and that the messages of different prophets and messengers must be congruent if they are claimed to be of divine authority. Since Muḥammad is regarded as the last of the prophets, it goes without saying that his message is the purest of them all, since no corruption could take place at the very moment when Muḥammad speaks on behalf of God. Furthermore, since the Qur'an is regarded as the account of divine speech sent down to Muḥammad, the Qur'an is also considered to be the pure divine word. Therefore all passages in other scriptures that contradict the Qur'anic understanding are deemed to be false. Ḥimāiyah follows this exact pattern of thought.

4.6.2.3. The One Common Ground and the One Choice to Be Made

It might seem at first blush as if the famous claim of common ground between the Muslim and Christian understandings would open up a space of free and impartial consideration. But upon closer inspection, it turns out that this is not the case. The reason is that the so-called "common" ground" is an "Islamic ground" from the very beginning because it rests on the assumption that Christians could by no means have a different revelation to the one testified to in the Qur'an. Therefore, to share in this common ground would entail accepting the Muslim conditions for dialogue. This option would automatically lead to the conclusion that the Qur'anic message is the true measure and standard for all claims of religious truth, no matter who uttered them. Accepting this common ground would thus inevitably mean that one has to embrace the Qur'anic message and therefore convert to Islam. This is what the *da'wah* hermeneutic is all about.

4.7. What Kind of Comparison Is This? – Some Critical Remarks

We return now to Ḥimāiyah's claimed attempt to compare different religions. The question is whether the "comparison of religions" he presents actually deserves that appellation. What kind of comparison does his book in fact provide? Before dealing with Ḥimāiyah's approach, let us begin with some remarks concerning the topic of comparison of religions in general.

4.7.1. Different Aspects to the Comparison of Religions

There is an ongoing debate about the prerequisite principles for a proper comparison between different religions. Some of these principles are rather simple – for instance, one should not compare the religious *ideals* of one religion (mostly to be found in its holy scriptures) with the somewhat disillusioning *praxis actually characterizing the day-to-day life* of another religion, since this necessarily leads to a biased view. Furthermore, one should avoid comparing entire religions with each other; instead, one should confine oneself to certain aspects or dimensions of the religious traditions in question. One should seek to compare things of the same dimension with each other; one should explain religious phenomena within their own context; one should consider one's own preferences, limitations (for instance in terms of language), blind spots, and so forth.[58] Unfortunately, our spatial limitations will allow us to deal with only some of these aspects here.

4.7.1.1. What Kind of Phenomena Could Be Compared between Different Religions?

Many scholars have stressed the fact that an overly simple comparison leads the observer astray. It is tempting, for instance, to select Jesus Christ and Muḥammad as the two phenomena to be considered when comparing Christianity and Islam, but a closer look reveals that it would be more appropriate to compare Jesus Christ with the Qur'an, since the operative question here is that of *revelation*. Similarly, it might seem cogent to compare the Bible with the Qur'an, since both are viewed as holy scriptures; however, Christians believe that the Bible witnesses to Jesus Christ as the incarnation of the divine logos, the essence of the revelation of God, while the Qur'an for its part claims to be of divine origin and an at least partial earthly manifestation of the *mother of the book* (*umm al-kitāb* in Arabic), a compendium of knowledge believed to be in the presence of God. Does Ḥimāiyah's comparison account for these differences (see 4.7.2.1)?

4.7.1.2. What Is the Actual Meaning Religious Actors Intend to Express?

To compare different religious teachings, it is necessary to inquire into the meaning of these teachings. Buddhist teachings, for example, are primarily intended to serve the purpose of achieving progress in meditation. The teachings are not a goal in and of themselves; rather, they serve as a boat helping the student to cross a river but are not meant to be of importance beyond that specific purpose. The same can be said of the Christian doctrine of the Trinity. It was not developed in order to define the mystery of God. Rather, it was meant to avoid misunderstandings about Jesus, the Christ, the Son of God.

Yet the authors we have been dealing with leave aside the historical circumstances that led to the formulation of Trinitarian dogma. Again: The intention was not to define the mystery of God, but *to avoid misinterpretations of the Christ event*. Jürgen Moltmann rightly states:

> The patristic doctrine of the Trinity does not originate in an absorption of the philosophical doctrine of the Logos, and of neo-Platonic triadologies, as has often been maintained. Its source is to be found in the New Testament witness to the Trinitarian history of the Son, and in the church's practice of baptism in the name of the triune God.

---

[58] Udo Tworuschka, "Das Vergleichen von Religionen," in Ulrich Becker and Udo Tworuschka, eds., *Ökumene und Religionswissenschaft* (Stuttgart: Calwer, 2006), 139-147.

> The early church's doctrine of the Trinity took on form during its resistance against dangerous heresies, in which the unity of Christ with God was called into question, either on God's behalf or on Christ's. It was only in these controversies that Trinitarian dogma grew up; and with the dogma grew its formulation, as philosophical terminology was given a new theological mold.
>
> The necessary resistance against Arianism on the one hand, and the laborious surmounting of Sabellianism on the other, led to the development of an explicit doctrine of the Trinity. Both heresies are christological in nature. Consequently, the dogma of the Trinity was evolved out of christology. It is designed to preserve faith in Christ, the son of God, and to direct the Christian hope towards full salvation in the divine fellowship. The doctrine of the Trinity cannot therefore be termed "a speculation." On the contrary, it is the theo logical premise for christology and soteriology.[59]

The question we must ask here is whether Ḥimāiyah considers this historical background to the development of Christian doctrine during the time of the ancient church. Does he recognize the intention of this Christian dogmatic tradition (see. 4.7.2.2)?

4.7.1.3. Which Context Provides the Right Framework to Explain a Religious Phenomenon?

On the one hand, the religious phenomenon Ḥimāiyah speaks to is the textual basis of Christian tradition, that is, the New Testament in its current form with its 27 individual books and as a whole. On the other hand, Ḥimāiyah also attempts to analyze the Christian doctrine of the Trinity by tracing this doctrine back to the scriptures of the Bible and by asking whether this doctrine appears to be "reasonable." In addition, he makes assumptions about where the doctrine of the Trinity might have come from, that is, the religious background from which this teaching might have been taken. The question then is whether Ḥimāiyah tries to understand what "Holy Scripture" means according to the Christian understanding, whether he tries to understand every New Testament scripture in its own way, whether he considers other ancient sources as well, and if so, whether he is able personally to translate all these scriptures after reading them in their original languages – ancient Greek, ancient Hebrew, Aramaic, Coptic, and so forth. This is, after all, a basic requirement for genuinely scholarly work (see 4.7.2.3).

4.7.1.4. Does the Author Attempt to Concede to the Other Religion a Logic of Its Own?

Even though it is a risky enterprise to compare whole religious traditions with each other, it is nevertheless indispensable for scholars to attempt to ascertain the

---

[59] Jürgen Moltmann, *The Trinity and the Kingdom: The Doctrine of God*, trans. Margaret Kohl (San Francisco: Harper, 1991), 129.

particular inherent logic of a religious phenomenon and of a religion as such. Such an attempt would require scholars to concede that a foreign religion might have a kind of coherence and an internal logic. Even if the scholar personally does not approve of this internal logic, it is nevertheless her scholarly obligation to search for it. Anthropologically speaking, it is neither plausible nor likely that a religious tradition is devoid of such an internal logic. The question therefore in the case before us is whether Ḥimāiyah demonstrates the attitude to concede to the Christian doctrinal tradition (specifically, the teaching of the Trinity) an internal logic and a more or less coherent worldview (see 4.7.2.4).

4.7.1.5. Does the Author Allow for the Possibility of Being Questioned by the Other Tradition?

After a scholar has analyzed a religious tradition and has written an account of it, the question remains whether she leaves room for being questioned by this same tradition in return. Even though the scholar might not agree with the internal logic, practical aspects, or cultural-religious heritages of that religion, it might still be possible for her to find something that makes sense to her – a new insight, for instance, or a different view of her own tradition, or something of that nature. Is there any indication that Ḥimāiyah regards the Christian doctrine as something by which to be challenged or inspired (see 4.7.2.5)?

4.7.2. Ḥimāiyah's Approach to Muqāranat al-Adyān

In the following section, we will put these five questions to Ḥimāiyah's book. Before we do so, however, we need to ask what Ḥimāiyah understands under the term *comparison of religions*, or *muqāranat al-adyān* in Arabic. Ḥimāiyah served as professor for the comparison of religions and was in fact the head of the comparison of religions department of the al-Azhar University branch in Asyut. Therefore, he played a key role in this field of study. *Therefore, the question as to the kind of comparison of religions Ḥimāiyah represents is of great importance.* Since Ḥimāiyah was responsible for the education of future Islamic personnel serving either in governmental administration, schooling, or higher education, his approach to the comparison of religions therefore has far-reaching consequences. Does Ḥimāiyah meet the basic standards for comparative religion as taught in most other countries?

4.7.2.1. The Qur'an as the Sole Paradigm of "Scripture"

As we have shown, Ḥimāiyah questions the validity of many passages in the New Testament scriptures. He values some New Testament books more highly, such as the Gospels of Mark, Matthew and Luke, and other books more critically, such as the Gospel of John and especially the letters of Paul. Again and again, he tries to show that the books of the New Testament are full of inconsistencies and errors. In doing so, it becomes obvious that Ḥimāiyah is applying his Islamic understanding of "scripture" to the Christian texts. According to Islamic understanding, the Qur'anic text was sent down part by part (*tanzīl* in Arabic) upon the prophet Muḥammad. The sole author of the scripture is God, whose messages are textually pure and absolutely coherent. The prophet Muḥammad has simply to deliver the fixed text. Muḥammad therefore has no influence on the divine message.

In applying this understanding to all the other prophets, including 'Īsā (Jesus), the author concludes that the books of the New Testament must be corrupted, having been distorted by Christians in the centuries after the coming of 'Īsā. Every textual difference therefore is seen as a proof of this distortion, even though not all of the textual material is distorted, as the Qur'an says. Arguing and analyzing from this perspective, Ḥimāiyah is not able to concede that the Christian understanding of the New Testament may be different. Christians generally regard the books of the New Testament as accounts by different human witnesses, even though they value the New Testament as inspired by the Holy Spirit. That means that the dimension of the human witness is itself part of what is called the Holy Bible. Unlike the Muslim understanding of the Qur'anic text as authored solely by God, the Christian understanding of the Bible views human witnesses as having been chosen by God to give accounts of the Christ event. Thus according to Christians, differences in the text are not proof of distortion, but an expression of the rich testimony given by the first Christians.

In applying his Islamic understanding of scripture to Christian sources, Ḥimāiyah is not attempting to understand the different books of the New Testament according to their own narrative. He does not regard the demarcations of a single book as the context of interpretation. Therefore, he deals merely with individual verses, instead of attempting to grasp the main idea of a particular book of the New Testament. Ḥimāiyah thus undertakes comparison of religions on the basis of Islamic doctrines only. He in no way seeks to understand Christian traditions according to their own self-understanding. This has far-reaching consequences for a number of other questions as well.

4.7.2.2. A Metaphysical "Ontology" as Yardstick of Interpretation

Since Ḥimāiyah does not try to understand the narrative of any one particular New Testament book, it is not at all surprising that his considerations concerning the Christian doctrine of the Trinity are not based on observations of the New Testament texts. Instead, he applies metaphysical categories to the texts. He regards the divine in a substantialist manner. That is to say, if the divine is seen as a kind of substance, then it makes sense to raise critical questions like: How can three distinct beings be called one? Furthermore, the author uses metaphysical categories to describe the divine, such as invisibility, omniscience, or omnipotence, and he does so in order to refute the Christian doctrine of the Trinity. These categories then serve as the yardstick for his interpretation of individual verses. But Ḥimāiyah does not consider the storyline or main ideas of whole New Testament books as such. This leads to rather simplistic conclusions – for instance, that the Christ could not be called God because he is visible.

The author obviously refuses to consider the main idea in the Christian understanding of God, namely the idea that God reveals himself in the *relational events* between God the Father, Jesus of Nazareth as the Son, and the Holy Spirit. Ḥimāiyah does not even tentatively attempt to track the Christian understanding. Therefore, his observations merely amount to the assertion that the doctrine of the Trinity is irrational. In no way does Ḥimāiyah consider that the doctrine of the Trinity was developed to distinguish the Christian understanding of Jesus Christ, true man and true God, from misinterpretations and heresies. The doctrine of the Trinity was meant and still is meant to draw a line between what *cannot* be said about Jesus Christ, the Son of God, and what must be confessed about him. The issue at stake here is Christology, and the doctrine of the Trinity is meant to circumscribe the mystery of God's revelation in Jesus Christ and in the power of the Holy Spirit.

In omitting the historical background of the doctrine of the Trinity and the intention of this doctrinal teaching, Ḥimāiyah shows that he is not actually interested in understanding what the doctrine is all about. Instead, he adheres to a purely Islamic understanding and does not show any ability to suspend his Islamic point of view. Yet this is exactly what is needed in order to achieve a proper comparison of different religions. The question then remains as to whether Ḥimāiyah's attempt should actually be called a comparison of religions at all.

4.7.2.3. Isolated Verses as the Object of Comparison

As mentioned above, Ḥimāiyah does not interpret the different verses he quotes within their own textual context. Instead, he strips quoted verses of their context. They simply serve as fodder for the argument he tries to make. Ḥimāiyah's book contains no references to exegetical works by Christian scholars, even though there has been and still is a an inordinate amount of vibrant scholarly work on New Testament exegesis available. The sources Ḥimāiyah does quote are old, dating back to the first half of the 19th century. A thorough comparison of religions would call for a representative selection of current exegetical work to be considered. In fact, the author demonstrates no knowledge of such work and no linguistic skills such as proficiency in or even familiarity with the ancient Greek or Hebrew languages at all. A comparison undertaken without the application of such skills would seem very shallow indeed.

4.7.2.4. Viewing the Other Religion as False, Irrational, Dishonest, and Childish

Even though Ḥimāiyah claims to approach the Christian tradition respectfully, his book shows an increasing tendency to judge Christian scriptures as corrupted and Christian doctrines as distortions. As a reminder, the author states in his preface: "Our book deals with the doctrine of Trinity on the basis of Christian sources and holy books. I try to present them carefully and honestly, without going beyond them or misrepresenting their beliefs."[60] And as we have seen, the author also concludes the book in an almost hostile manner:

[60] Ḥimāiyah, *Taṯlīṯ*, Preface (no numbering).

> The Christian religion was built on the basis of pure and reasonable monotheism, but they turned it into a religion of idolatry by establishing an unreasonable Trinity, taken from the Trinity of the Greeks and the Romans, quoted from the Trinity of the Egyptians and Brahmins in a distorted quote. Taking a religion of heavenly law, they recreated its entire law by abolishing it and replacing it with innovations (arab. *bidaʿ*) and traditions alien to it. A religion of ascetism, modesty, austerity, altruism, and servanthood (arab. *ʿabūdīya*), and they turned it into a religion of greed and desire, luxury, selfish-ness and enslavement of human beings.[61]

Tellingly, the author does not warrant or substantiate these various accusations. They simply amount to general claims that the Christian religion makes people become greedy, prideful, and the like. In all of his reflections, Ḥimāiyah tries to show that Christian doctrine is irrational, false, and dishonest. So the question remains: Does the author seriously believe that he is treating the Christian traditions with respect and that he is attempting to understand them *according to their own logic*? This is obviously not the case, as shown above. Therefore, the basic prerequisites for a comparison of religions according to scholarly standards are not given, even though Ḥimāiyah claims in his preface to deal with the issues in a "scholarly manner": "I order the evidence and the arguments and proceed by way of scholarly investigation, drawing on the most correct and documented sources."[62]

This leads to the conclusion that when the author believes his approach to the comparison of religions to be scholarly, he defines that to mean interpreting and pronouncing judgment on another religious tradition (in this case, the Christian tradition) solely on the basis of the standards of his own religion (Islam). In European contexts, this type of approach would be called apologetical at best.

4.7.2.5. A One-sided, Supersessionary Approach

The author adheres to the main ideas of the Qur'anic view of other religions, that is, that other religions have been superseded by Islam and that they need to be corrected until they conform to the doctrines of Islam. This approach is one-sided, inasmuch as it does not believe other religious traditions to have any value of their own.

To conclude: This approach should be respected as a theological statement, but it hardly counts as a scholarly one, at least not in the sense that academic faculties and scholarly communities in most other countries would define "scholarly" – not even broadly speaking.

It would appear that Ḥimāiyah's claim to deal with another religious tradition in a "scholarly manner" is an attempt to appear trustworthy. Readers not acquainted with either of these religious traditions (Christianity and Islam) may find his deliberations helpful in some ways, but his book certainly does not serve as an example of a proper comparison of religions.

---

[61] Ḥimāiyah, *Taṯlīṯ*, 75.

[62] Ḥimāiyah, *Taṯlīṯ*, Preface (no numbering).

4.7.3. Prospects and Questions: What Kind of Scholarly Work Is Being Done at Al-Azhar?

All of these observations prompt us to ask whether Ḥimāiyah as a scholar is an exception, or whether he typifies the way of thinking of Islamic scholars at al-Azhar University. And if the latter is true, Western readers may well ask how to deal with this phenomenon.

4.7.3.1. Evaluating Christian Traditions Independently of the Qur'anic View?

Ḥimāiyah's way of comparing religions in his book has shown that he adheres to the Qur'anic understanding of Christian traditions, along with all the limitations inevitably given by this approach. It has become clear that this is not a viable approach to understanding Christianity the way it understands itself. Therefore, the challenge for Islamic scholarship is to be willing to suspend the Qur'anic understanding of Christianity in order to grasp the internal logic of Christian sources.

4.7.3.2. The Possibility of Accepting Insights of Western Scholarship

This raises the question whether the author would be willing to accept Western scholarship on Biblical texts. It is reasonable to assume that Ḥimāiyah would suspect such an approach of weakening the Qur'anic understanding of Christians and Christianity. Since Western exegetical scholarship applies a "secular" methodology to Christian texts, this might however offer a way forward. Such an approach would not deal with the question whether the texts themselves should be regarded as true or false, but with the question as to what the logic of a particular text (such as a particular New Testament book) is. The outcome might be that even though Muslims would deem the content to be false, they might nevertheless appreciate the internal logic of the text as coherent, lucid, or meaningful.

4.7.3.3. Studying Christian Sources Using the Original Languages

This would lead to the additional challenge of learning the original languages in which Christian source texts were written, in order to understand them appropriately. Since Muslim scholarship of the Qur'an demands mastery of the Arabic language, this should not be an unreasonable requirement in return. It would be an important step towards mutual understanding if al-Azhar would not only establish faculties for modern foreign languages like English, French, or German, but also faculties for the study of the languages of other religious traditions like Sanskrit, ancient Greek, or ancient Hebrew.

4.7.3.4. Evaluating the Internal Logic of Different Religious Traditions

Comparing the internal logic of different faiths or religious traditions might not lead to the discovery of similarities with regard to religious positions, but it certainly would show similarities in the operative mindset and reflections on religious matters. Even though different religions operate with different mindsets, the underlying philosophical questions are similar. Examples include the question as to the extent to which human language is capable of representing transcendent matters. Comparing approaches to such questions would not be about trying to convince the Other of a particular viewpoint, but about joint efforts of reflection.

4.7.3.5. Understanding the Real Differences – And Tolerating Them

Instead of simply engaging in apologetics, fulfilling these various stipulations would constitute an important step towards mutual understanding of the *real differences* between different religious and ideological traditions. Even though all participants are free to maintain their own convictions, this approach would lead to the insight that human beings share the same challenges in expressing their belief or worldview. This would amount to an important first step towards mutual appreciation.

5. Ṭāhā Rayyān (b. 1939)

5.1. Biographical Overview

'Alī Ṭāhā Rayyān was born in Luxor, Egypt in 1939. He memorized the Qur'an as a child already. After attending al-Azhar schools in Upper Egypt, he received his Bachelor's Degree from the al-Azhar *Faculty of Sharia and Law* (*sharia wa kanūn* in Arabic) in 1966 and his Master's Degree from the same faculty in 1968. He completed his doctoral dissertation in 1973, entitled: "Comparative Jurisprudence" (*muqāranat al fiqh* in Arabic). He held the rank of assistant professor in the *Faculty of Sharia and Law* from 1980 until 1985. In 1982, he was appointed dean of the *Faculty of Sharia and Law* at the al-Azhar branch of Asyut. In 1996, he was appointed vice president of al-Ahqaf University in Yemen. From 2000 to 2004, he headed the *Comparative Jurisprudence Department* of the *Faculty of Sharia and Law* in Cairo. Throughout the 1980s and 1990s, he also taught at universities all over the world, including Umm al-Qura University in Medina, as well as in countries such as Pakistan, Bangladesh, Tunisia, Uzbekistan, and the United States, to mention but a few.

Ṭāhā Rayyān has published a number of books. The topics comprise themes of Islamic law, the interpretation of Islamic sources like the Ḥadīth, comparisons between different schools of law, and others. He released a number of fatwas via different media. Several of these fatwas can be viewed on YouTube. Ṭāhā Rayyān has also written on the question of other religions, especially Christianity.[1]

5.2. Rayyān's Book "The Messiah, Son of Mary, in the Holy Qur'an"

The following analysis will focus on Ṭāhā Rayyān's book: *The Messiah, Son of Mary, in the Holy Qur'an*. It was published in Arabic as *Al Masīḥ ibn Maryam fī al-qur'ān al karīm* in 2013. We will begin by providing an overview of the content. That will be followed by some observations about the author's methodology.

5.2.1. Dedication and Content

Rayyān's book comprises 257 pages. It is divided into 22 sections, each of which deals with a different topic. The author addresses these topics using passages of

---

[1] Al-Azhar University, www.azhar.eg/m-alazhar/kibar-alolamaa/ (accessed July 15, 2019).

the Qur'an. These passages are taken from only 12 Surahs, especially Surahs 2, 3, 4, 5, and 19. The book begins with an introduction and ends with a conclusion.

Rayyān prefaces his work with a dedication. It reads: ""Dedication. To all Christians all over the world from different denominations, beliefs, and doctrines, and even to secularists of them ... To those searching for the truth and for faith, to rational people and to the wise searching for ... a way of success."[2] This dedication is interesting for several reasons. Firstly, it is directed to all Christians worldwide. This means that the author deems his work to be important for all of Christianity. Secondly, Rayyān groups these Christians with seekers of the truth, instead of recognizing them as people who believe they have already received the truth. In this way, the author implies that Christians are still searching for the truth as well. Thirdly, the author associates the question of truth and faith with the topic of rational thinking and wisdom. This implies that truth can be found using rational thinking. Fourthly, Rayyān implies that his book will enable people to find the way to salvation which is granted in Islam.

The dedication is followed by an introduction. Before proceeding to analyze the introduction, we should first give an overview of the content of the book. The table of contents reveals the order of thinking. Rayyān's ideas can be outlined by simply giving the headings for the chapters in the order of the book. It reads as follows (page numbers are provided directly after each heading for ease of reference):

(1) *The Beginning of the Book* (Surah 1:1-7) (pp. 8-14);

(2) *Adam's Sin* (Surah 2:30-39) (pp. 15-23);

(3) *The Religion of Ibrahim* (Surah 2:130-140) (pp. 24-29);

(4) *The Birth of Yahya* (Surah 19:1-15) (pp. 30-36);

(5) *The Miracle of the Birth of Christ* (Surah 19:16-40) (pp. 37-44);

(6) *A Claim Almost Collapses the Universe* (Surah 19:88-98) (pp. 45-47);

(7) *The Religion of Allah* (Surah 3:1-32) (pp. 48-80);

(8) *Come to a Common Word* (Surah 3:33-64) (pp. 81-103);

(9) *The Truth of Prophecy and Message* (Surah 3:78-91) (pp. 104-111);

(10) *The Position of the Jews towards Christ* (Surah 4:150-159) (pp. 112-119);

(11) *Rabbis and Monks* (Surah 9:30-35) (pp. 120-132);

(12) *Different Denominations on the Nature of Christ* (Surah 43:57-89) (pp. 133-145);

(13) *Facts and Destinies* (Surah 91:1-8) (pp. 146-153);

(14) *They are Disbelievers Who Believe that Christ is the Son of God* (Surah 5:14-19)
(pp. 154-163);

(15) *The Judge of Sharia* (Surah 5:44-50) (pp. 164-176);

(16) *They are Disbelievers Who Believe that God has Three Persons* (Surah 5:65-77)
(pp. 177-195);

(17) *The True Faith* (Surah 5:78-86) (pp. 196-207);

(18) *The Messiah: Servant and Messenger of God* (Surah 5:109-120) (pp. 208-217);

[2] 'Alī Ṭāhā Rayyān, *Al Masīḥ ibn Maryam fī al-qur'ān al karīm* (Cairo 2013), 2.

(19) *Call Christians to Monotheism* (Surah 4:171-175) (pp. 218-228);
(20) *The Gospel of Christ* (Surah 69:5-14) (pp. 229-240);
(21) *Names and Attributes of God* (Surah 59:16-24) (pp. 241-246);
(22) *Monotheism* (Surah 112) (pp. 247-251);
Conclusion (pp. 252-257).

The table of contents already signals Rayyān's methodology.

5.2.2. The Introduction of the Book – References to Methodology

We will analyze the table of contents below. First, however, we should consider the introduction. Rayyān begins by stressing the importance of doctrine for the universe, history, human life in this world, and the hereafter.[3] So he believes that doctrine should be taken seriously, and the reason he gives is that doctrine is not simply a tradition or a heritage from the fathers; rather, people's minds should be convinced of the faith. This, he believes, will enlighten the heart and provide guidance in life.

This brings the author to address a Christian audience about the purpose of his book: "This research is a call to Christians – from all denominations – to enter the religion of God that all the messengers came with." A quotation of Surah 21:25 follows.[4] Rayyān underscores the importance of the Qur'an. Doctrine was given in the Surahs of Mecca, he argues, while in the Surahs of Medina the law and a system for life was given.[5]

After these preliminary statements Rayyān turns to the question of the reliability of the Qur'an: "God the Almighty ensures that the 'Holy Qur'an' is preserved from distortion and addition and subtraction and alteration and all forms and kinds of tampering."[6] He states that since Muḥammad is the seal of the prophets, that is, the last prophet, the Qur'an is also the seal of the religions. Rayyān quotes a number of verses in support of his assertions, such as Surah 21:107 and 33:40. He goes on to explain that he has chosen passages from the Qur'an in order to answer questions about Christ and provide a clear picture of Christ. He also refers to Sayyid Quṭb and his legendary commentary on the Qur'an, entitled *In the Shadow of the Qur'an*.[7]

Next, Rayyān quotes Surah 2:256 to argue that while there is "no compulsion in religion," it is the duty of Muslims to convey the message of the Qur'an to all the people of the world. He writes: "This Qur'an does not favor anyone and does not oppress anyone. The Qur'an sets the standards and conditions of faith. Those who fulfill its conditions are the believers, and whoever does not meet them is not a believer."[8] Rayyān ends the introduction with a quotation from Surah 29:69: "But

---

[3] Rayyān, *Al Masīḥ*, 5.
[4] Rayyān, *Al Masīḥ*, 5.
[5] Rayyān, *Al Masīḥ*, 6.
[6] Rayyān, *Al Masīḥ*, 6.
[7] Rayyān, *Al Masīḥ*, 6.
[8] Rayyān, *Al Masīḥ*, 7.

We shall be sure to guide to Our ways those who strive hard for Our cause: God is with those who do good."[9]

The introduction shows that the author believes it is sufficient to refer only or primarily to Qur'anic texts, since these texts – as words of God – have the power to convince the reader of the truth. Furthermore, he claims that the Qur'anic text does not favor anybody at the expense of anybody else. This implies that Rayyān in a certain sense ascribes to the Qur'anic text a neutral character. Since he considers the Qur'anic text to be the divine truth, the text itself – in a way – functions as a means of comparison.

Even though Rayyān implicitly argues for a certain kind of neutrality, his approach rests entirely on Islamic assumptions. We will enumerate at least seven of them: He assumes, firstly, that the divine text is not corrupted in any way; secondly, that the divine text has the power to convince the reader; thirdly, that whatever truth claim anybody makes has to be judged by the Qur'anic text; fourthly, that the comparison he undertakes is intended to clarify misunderstandings; fifthly, that the ultimate goal is to lead people on the path of salvation, that is, to Islam; sixthly, that anyone applying proper reasoning will assent to the arguments of the Qur'an; and, seventhly, that the Qur'an is not distorted, whereas the scriptures of other religions (especially, the Jewish and Christian religions) are indeed distorted.

We now return to the analysis of the table of contents and its line of thinking.

5.2.3. The Line of Thinking Reflected in the Table of Contents – An Interpretation

Our aim here is to consider and reflect upon the author's main ideas as reflected in the table of contents. Admittedly, the table of contents can be interpreted in different ways; even so, our interpretation is an attempt to understand the theological logic behind the selection of Qur'anic verses undertaken by Rayyān. Chapter numbers will be indicated in brackets.

5.2.3.1. Islamic Anthropology as Opposed to Christian Claims

The author starts chapter 1 with some general remarks on *al-fatiha*, the first Surah of the Qur'an. In chapter 2, he expands on Islamic anthropology. With reference to Surah 2:30-39, he argues that there is an "eternal battlefield" between good and evil, between God and Satan,[10] and that Adam's sin consisted of his refusal to obey the will of God. Thankfully, God forgave him, and since then, it is the duty of human beings to obey the will of God.

An important point for Rayyān is the Islamic anthropological claim that every human being is responsible for himself – that is to say, for his own deeds only. He

[9] Rayyān, *Al Masīḥ*, 7. It should be noted that all quotations from the Qur'an in this study are drawn from the following translation: *The Qur'an*, trans. M.A.S. Abdel Haleem. Oxford World's Classics. Oxford: Oxford University Press, 2005.

[10] Rayyān, *Al Masīḥ*, 18.

states: “Sin is individual. … There is no sin imposed on man before his birth.”[11] Here Rayyān is referring to the teachings of the church concerning original sin and atonement. He rejects both of these teachings. It is noteworthy that in doing so, he does not provide any references from the Christian scriptures nor from Christian theology at all.

Next, Rayyān moves to the topic of *The Religion of Ibrahim* (3), *The Birth of Yahya* (commonly identified as John the Baptist) (4), and the birth of ‘Īsā (5). Taken together, chapters 1-5 amount to a counter picture to the Christian understanding of original sin and the redeeming activity of Christ. In his interpretation of Surah 19:38-40, Rayyān reaffirms the Islamic view that ‘Īsā is simply a prophet.[12]

5.2.3.2. The Turning Point

The next chapter is entitled *A Claim Almost Collapses the Universe* (6). It can be seen as a kind of turning point for the book, since the author now argues that the claim that God has a son or any child at all is perverse. Even though this chapter is not explicitly directed against Christian teachings, it is evidently to be understood in this way. In his interpretation of Surah 19:88-98, Rayyān stresses that the abovementioned claim concerns the entire universe. He emphasizes that the claim is false and to be avoided under all circumstances.

5.2.3.3. The True Religion and a Common Word

After this general theological statement, Rayyān proceeds with three topics, that is (7) the *Religion of Allah* (Surah 3:1-32); (8) *Come to a Common Word* (Surah 3:33-64); and (9) *The Truth of Prophecy and Message* (Surah 3:78-91). Having dealt, firstly, with Islamic anthropology, and, secondly, with the false claim that God has begotten a son or a child, the author now, thirdly, argues for the true understanding which to him is the understanding of God as being the one and only God over against the world. Rayyān affirms that Islam is the religion of God and quotes Surah 3:64, which calls all people to come together for a common word. Now the actual content of this common word is the call to embrace Islam. The last sentence in Rayyān’s chapter on this topic (8) clearly calls all human beings to Islam as *the* religion of God.[13]

5.2.3.4. The Rejection of False Truth Claims

The next seven chapters are devoted to the rejection of truth claims attributed to Jews and Christians. The chapters are entitled: (10) *The Position of the Jews towards Christ* (Surah 4:150-159); (11) *Rabbis and Monks* (Surah 9:30-35); (12) *Different Denominations on the Nature of Christ* (Surah 43:57-89); (13) *Facts and Destinies* (Surah 91:1-8); (14) *They are Disbelievers Who Believe that Christ is the Son of God* (Surah 5:14-19); (15) *The Judge of Sharia* (Surah 5:44-50); and (16)

---

[11] Rayyān, *Al Masīḥ*, 22.

[12] Rayyān, *Al Masīḥ*, 38-42.

[13] Rayyān, *Al Masīḥ*, 103.

They are Disbelievers Who Believe that God has Three Persons (Surah 5:65-77). We will speak to these chapters in detail below.

5.2.3.5. The True Understanding of 'Īsā Ibn Maryam

Rayyān goes on in chapters 17-20 to unfold an Islamic understanding of 'Īsā ibn Maryam (Jesus, the son of Mary). The chapters are entitled as follows: (17) *The True Faith* (Surah 5:78-86); (18) *Christ Is a Servant and an Apostle of God* (Surah 5:109-120); (19) *Call Christians to Monotheism* (Surah 4:171-175); and (20) *The Gospel of Christ* (Surah 69:5-14). It is important to note that this section not only aims to develop an Islamic understanding of 'Īsā ibn Maryam, but also to argue that it is the duty of all Muslims to call others to Islam.

5.2.3.6. Islam as the True Religion – Final Remarks

The author concludes his book with the following three chapters: (21) *Names and Attributes of God* (Surah 59:16-24); (22) *Monotheism* (Surah 112); and the *Conclusion*. This final section serves to repeat and reinforce the Islamic truth claim. We will have more to say about Rayyān's conclusion below.

5.2.3.7. Summary of Rayyān's Line of Thinking

The unique contribution of the book *The Messiah, Son of Mary, in the Holy Qur'an* consists of two things: firstly, in its particular selection of Qur'anic verses, and, secondly, in its ordering of these verses. Rayyān's interpretations typically affirm the content of the Qur'anic texts.

Our overview of the table of contents implies that Rayyān's line of thinking may be compared with a kind of medical anamnesis and the restoration of health. Firstly, he speaks about the true religion, which corresponds to the state of healthy human beings. Secondly, he outlines the problems of a perverted or distorted understanding of God, the way a doctor might speak about a health problem, in this case as a departure from the healthy knowledge potentially inherent to all human beings. Thirdly, he discusses the problem in detail, the way a medical specialist might analyze a sickness, in this case as a forgetting or "anamnesis" of healthy knowledge. Fourthly, he portrays the true understanding of God as a doctor might prescribe medical treatment for the sick, here specifically as a return to or regaining of healthy knowledge. Fifthly, and finally, he describes the true religion as a restoration of the state of health.

5.3. A Selection of Topics from *The Messiah, Son of Mary, in the Holy Qur'an*

A selection of topics from the book will provide us with enough examples to show how the Rayyān approaches the comparison of religions. The selected examples to be discussed in this section are sufficiently representative, since he again and again argues in the same way.

5.3.1. The Trinity as a Distorted Teaching

In chapter sixteen, entitled "*They are Disbelievers* [*kufr* in Arabic] *Who Believe that God has Three Persons*," Rayyān attempts to refute the doctrine of the Trinity (p. 177-195). He begins the chapter by quoting Surah 5:65-77. Among other things, this passage of the Qur'an says that if the People of the Book were to be pious and obey what God has sent down to them, then God would be merciful with them and would provide them with food (5:65-66). The following verses raise claims the Qur'an makes about the People of the Book. Surah 5:72-73 reads:

> Those who say, 'God is the Messiah, son of Mary,' have defied God. The Messiah himself said, 'Children of Israel, worship God, my Lord and your Lord.' If anyone associates [*yushrik* in Arabic] others with God, God will forbid him from the Garden, and Hell will be his home. No one will help such evildoers. Those people who say that God is the third of three are defying [the truth] [*laqad kafara* in Arabic]: there is only One God. If they persist in what they are saying, a painful punishment will afflict those of them who persist.

5.3.1.1. Follow the Method of God to Benefit in this Life and the Next

After repeating Surah 5:65-66, Rayyān goes on in chapter 16 to argue that people should follow "the method of God," and that if they do so, their life will prosper and there will be hope for them in the hereafter. Rayyān claims that the human mind today is shaken and that human beings are disturbed. Therefore they are in need of the clear guidance provided by the method of Allah. He states:

> If they follow the method of God [*manhaj allāh* in Arabic] found in the *Torah* and the *Injīl*, and the teachings God sent down to them – the way God sent them down, i.e. undistorted [*bidūn taḥrīf* in Arabic] and unchanged [*wa lā tabdīl* in Arabic] – then their life would become better in this world, provisions will increase and pour down upon them, and they will eat from above... [they will have] plenty of provisions, an increase of products, and excellent distribution, and matters of life will be resolved.[14]

The next ten pages deal with the topic of the right teaching. The author maintains that if the People of the Book were to set aside the false teachings found in the Biblical scriptures, they would not only get a proper understanding of God and the will of God, but in so doing they would also prosper. It is the Islamic system, based on the Qur'an, that makes life good and just (180), he claims; it is the Islamic method that guides human beings in life and to the hereafter (181), people

[14] Rayyān, *Al Masīḥ*, 178.

should stand up against disbelief and materialism (182) and against atheism (187), and they should unite under Islam.

This section amounts to an attempt on the part of the author to convince both the People of the Book and Muslims that following the method of Allah will enable human beings to live a good life ordered by the commands of God that help to improve life and give hope for the afterlife.

5.3.1.2. Avoid Distorted Teachings like the Divinity of Christ or the Trinity

At this point, Rayyān returns to the question of distorted teachings among Christians.[15] Concerning the Trinity, he contends that "the Christian authors of theology attempted to postpone rational consideration of this issue, which the mind rejects."[16] After having dealt with the question of the Trinity with just a few sentences, the author goes on to quote some Qur'anic verses he deems sufficient to refute Christian theological ideas. It should be noted that Rayyān does not address or discuss the logic of Christian theological arguments or New Testament texts as such, but that he contents himself with quoting verses like Surah 5:72-73, as mentioned above.

With regard to Surah 5:75, Rayyān states:

> Eating food was a real issue in the life of Christ – peace be upon him – and his friendly mother, specially characteristic of the events of his life, and an indication of the humanity of Christ and his mother. It is also to an extent a theological expression. Eating food is done to meet the needs of the body and soul – and there is no god who needs food to survive.[17]

This argument shows that Rayyān does not even attempt to understand Christian teachings according the texts of the New Testament or the theological concepts of Christian doctrine. He simply quotes Surah 5:77 to warrant that the People of the Book should not exceed the limits of truth in their religion.[18]

5.3.1.3. Rayyān's Line of Argument

It has become obvious that Rayyān is not interested in analyzing and evaluating Christian teachings. He does not quote New Testament texts, does not discuss Christian doctrines, does not consider Christian theologians, and does not take Christian exegesis into account. He does not even refer to Muslim exegetical commentaries, since he is convinced that the mere quotation of Qur'anic verses suffices to refute Christian teachings.

Rayyān's line of argument runs as follows: In the first part of the section, he invites the People of the Book to follow Qur'anic teachings and to judge their own

[15] Rayyān, *Al Masīḥ*, 191ff.
[16] Rayyān, *Al Masīḥ*, 192.
[17] Rayyān, *Al Masīḥ*, 193
[18] Rayyān, *Al Masīḥ*, 194.

scriptures according to the teachings of the Qur'an. If they do this, the Qur'an promises that the People of the Book will understand ultimate truth and thus have an opportunity to improve their life in this world and the next. That is to say, Rayyān promises that their life will improve not only in terms of matters of faith, but also – and concomitantly – in terms of material things like a good family life, an ample supply of the goods people need to live a good life, and hope for the hereafter. The basic contention is that if people embrace Islam, their life will improve.

In the second part of the chapter, Rayyān calls on the People of the Book to abandon certain distorted teachings. The line of argument in this part runs as follows: Firstly, Rayyān illustrates the positive results that come from following the method of Allah in order to invite Christians in particular to consider closely the message of the Qur'an. This section is a kind of advertisement. Secondly, he describes what Christians have to leave behind if they want to acquire the good life that comes from following the Qur'anic message and the method of God. In other words, he treats Christian content like New Testament texts or Christian doctrines *only as an obstacle*, arguing that such content makes it impossible for Christians to follow the method of God taught in the Qur'an.

5.3.2. The 'Īsā of the Qur'an as Opposed to What Christians Teach about Him

Chapter eighteen is entitled "*The Messiah: Servant and Messenger of God*" (p. 208-217). Rayyān begins the chapter by quoting Surah 5:109-120. This Qur'anic text is about 'Īsā, his miracles, his disciples, his mother, and other topics. Surah 5:116 reads:

> When God says, 'Jesus, son of Mary, did you say to people, "Take me and my mother as two gods alongside God"?' he will say, 'May You be exalted! I would never say what I had no right to say – if I had said such a thing You would have known it: You know all that is within me, though I do not know what is within You, You alone have full knowledge of things unseen.

The author then proceeds to comment on the verses of the text.

5.3.2.1. 'Īsā as Proof that Christian Claims Are False

Rayyān maintains that the scene of Surah 5:116 is that of Judgment Day. This day will come as shock to all human beings, since all truth will come to light.[19] In the following pages, the author deals with the different topics mentioned in Surah 5:109-120. His intention is to show that all these topics reveal that 'Īsā is only a human being and a messenger, nothing more. Furthermore, it is 'Īsā himself who answers God that he, 'Īsā, never even claimed to have a divine nature. Concerning

[19] Rayyān, *Al Masīḥ*, 209.

the story about the feast table 'Īsā asks God to send down from heaven in order to feed the disciples, Rayyān states that this story is not mentioned in the Biblical scriptures. Instead, there is a story in the Gospel of Matthew of 'Īsā feeding a large crowd of people by multiplying bread and fish.

The author does not argue; he simply asserts that there is at the very least a similarity between the accounts. He simply assumes that the Christian scriptures have been distorted, and so he does not even go into detail about the differences between the accounts.[20] Surah 5:109-120 reports a number of miracles as having been performed by 'Īsā but as done by God himself. Against this background, the author points out that Muḥammad is not reported to have done any similar miracles. Instead, he emphasizes that the Qur'an itself ought to be regarded as a miracle. Rayyān then tells the story of a Bosnian lady who attended a Friday prayer meeting which he held during a sea voyage to New York. He describes how she admitted that she did not understand the meaning of the words he said, but that the sound of the Arabic words made her cry. By telling this story, the author obviously intends to give an example illustrating the miracle of the Qur'an as a direct message from Allah.[21] His main argument in this section however is that *'Īsā himself* corrected – according to Surah 5:109-120 – false claims about his nature made by other people.

5.3.2.2. Commenting on the Qur'anic Text Instead of Proceeding by Way of Reasoning

In this chapter, Rayyān does not quote any Islamic sources other than the Qur'an. He quotes verse after verse and comments on them. Taken together, these comments do not amount to a reasoned argument as such, but simply to a kind of affirmation. Rayyān deems the Qur'anic text to be completely sufficient. There is no need for any kind of reasoned argumentation, since the Qur'an addresses the human mind and human reason. Even though Rayyān's intent is clearly apologetic, the tone of his comments is not aggressive, but rather affirmative.

5.3.2.3. Qur'anic Texts as Sufficient Proof of the Truth

It needs to be said explicitly that the author largely confines himself to quoting the Qur'an. There are almost no references to stories from the Ḥadīth tradition, nor any references to Islamic thinkers of the past and present. Therefore it is not surprising that Rayyān's book does not include a bibliography. He uses only a few sources. When venturing outside the Qur'an, he most often refers to Sayyid Quṭb, either simply mentioning him or quoting passages from his massive commentary, *In the Shade of the Qur'an.* In the rare references when the author refers to Quṭb and other authors, he only cites names without providing any bibliographical information. It is therefore impossible to confirm or disconfirm such references. Since Rayyān considers the Qur'anic text to be sufficient for his purposes, he does

[20] Rayyān, *Al Masīḥ*, 212.

[21] Rayyān, *Al Masīḥ*, 226.

not even quote Biblical texts. This observation naturally raises questions about his methodology.

5.4. Methodology

Tellingly, Taha Rayyān does not deal with questions of methodology as such. He simply starts by explaining that his book is addressed to Christians worldwide. It seems self-evident to the author that the Qur'anic text explains itself sufficiently.

5.4.1. Usage of Qur'anic Texts

Throughout the book, Rayyān gives no direct references to any Muslim or Christian thinkers. The book includes a number of Qur'anic texts, cited to match the order of topics he proposes. He believes that the message of the Qur'an criticizes and corrects Christian perceptions of, say, God, Christ, and the Trinity. Never once does Rayyān reflect on where and when particular passages of the Qur'an were sent down. This means that the author never refers to the discipline of the *asbāb an-nuzūl* (occasions or circumstances of the revelation of Qur'anic verses).

5.4.1.1. Texts without Any Historical Context

Rayyān is not interested in the historical circumstances of the revelation of the various Qur'anic texts. In contrast, Islamic exegesis in general tries to establish, firstly, on which occasion (historical event) a certain text was sent down to the messenger (Muḥammad), secondly, whom exactly the text addresses, and, thirdly, what the intention of the passage in question may be. Rayyān does not address any of these points. To him, the texts seem to be self-explanatory, having an eternal content that simply needs to be applied.

5.4.1.2. Passages without Textual Context

Furthermore, Rayyān is not concerned with the textual context of the passages he cites. There are no considerations of, for instance, the character of a particular Surah, no reflections about other passages where the same topic appears, where the same keywords appear, or the like. Instead, Rayyān cites passages as he pleases. He often selects short sentences from the Qur'an, to which he supplies lengthy explanations. The passages are simply used to underline his arguments.

5.4.1.3. First Consequence: Unspecified Addressees

Rayyān intends to explain to Christians what pure monotheism is according to the Qur'an. To this end, he selects a number of Qur'anic texts. Since he provides no details about the history behind the revelation of the texts nor about the textual context, it is unclear *to whom exactly* a particular passage is addressed. In other words, it is not clear whether the particular text addresses Arabic pagans, certain groups of Jews, Bedouins, individuals opposing the prophet, hypocrites in the prophet's own ranks, certain Christian groups, or "Christians" in general (a term he does not define either), or others. Rayyān essentially addresses all of his texts to Christians in general, as it were. There is no specification of the addressees.

5.4.1.4. Second Consequence: Labeling the Opponents

At this point, a problem arises: The Qur'anic texts clearly address different groups of people in different ways. The critique of the Qur'anic message over against Arabic paganism is different from its critique of different groups of Christians. By failing to factor in the historical circumstances behind the revelation of different Qur'anic passages, Rayyān intermingles the various answers. He generalizes the Qur'anic critique and in so doing applies points of critique to Christians that might have been addressed to Arabic paganism. In this way, Rayyān, firstly, fails to account for differences that are evident in the Qur'an, and in so doing, secondly, subsumes all Christians under the label of idolaters and polytheists, as his conclusion of the sixteenth chapter of his book reveals:

> The first thing is the fact that this great effort of the Islamic approach is directed at correcting misperceptions of faith. Established on the basis of absolute monotheism, its aim is the purification from the impurities of idolatry [*wathaniyya* in Arabic] and polytheism [*shirk* in Arabic] that corrupted the doctrines of the People of the Book.[22]

5.4.2. Usage of Other Sources

We have mentioned that in his book, Rayyān gives almost no references, largely quoting only Qur'anic verses. He certainly does not engage current Christian thought. Even though the book is intended to address Christians worldwide, there are only rare instances when the author actually says something about modern-day Christians. The book does include some considerations about atheism, but rarely about Christianity as such.

5.4.2.1. Omission of Christian Sources

The book's lack of references to New Testament or Biblical texts shows that the author is not concerned with the testimony of the Bible, nor does he show any knowledge of Christian theological debates, past and present. There are no names of famous Christian theologians to be found, nor any references to Christian exegesis and the like.

5.4.2.2. Omission of Christian Theology

Furthermore, Rayyān is not concerned with the theology of particular New Testament scriptures like the Gospels of Matthew, Mark, Luke, or John. There is no

---

[22] Rayyān, *Al Masīḥ*, 194.

attempt by Rayyān to outline even basic ideas of Christian doctrine, let alone any crucial developments of Christian history. Here and there one may find some intimations, but nothing more. In chapter 16, for example, the author simply states that Christians proposed a certain doctrine (Trinity), but then, as mentioned above, he immediately goes on to state that "the Christian authors of theology attempted to postpone rational consideration of this issue which the mind rejects."[23] This shows that the author himself does not intend to discuss these theological issues himself. He regards the theological issue as already solved through the message of the Qur'an.

5.4.2.3. Absence of Theological Reasoning

This observation leads to the question how Rayyān intends to reason with potential Christian readers. Does he actually expect any Christians to read his book at all? Or is his book merely meant to boost the self-confidence of a Muslim audience? The absence of theological reasoning shows that the author himself is not engaged in disputing different theological agendas. Rather, Rayyān is evidently very confident that the words of the Qur'anic message themselves will be sufficient to convince the readers.

5.4.3. Rayyān's Approach to the Comparison of Religions

Therefore, it appears that the author refrains from making comparisons at all, because he deems them to be of minor importance. The question arises: What kind of comparison of religions is at stake here?

5.4.3.1. The Comparison of Religions is Expected to be Undertaken by Christian Readers

By addressing Christians while referring only to Qur'anic texts, the author expects that Christians will come to certain conclusions merely by reading the Qur'anic verses. Since he believes that the Qur'an is in accordance with human reason and rationality, he contents himself with outlining the arguments of the Qur'an concerning human beings and their relation to Allah. Evidently, the idea is that by following Rayyān's main thoughts, as outlined by the arrangement of texts, Christian readers will be called upon to compare what they have believed hitherto with the arguments given in the Qur'an.

This kind of comparison is undertaken by readers who are called upon to consider their own biography and the teachings they have heard and adhered to so far. The intended comparison of religions is therefore an individual endeavor. The method employed by Rayyān assumes that the result of such a comparison between Christian teachings (Christ being the son of God, the Trinity, redemption, and others) and the Qur'anic message is already clear: That Christian teachings are false in a number of aspects, whereas the Qur'anic message is the pure and unadulterated truth.

[23] Rayyān, *Al Masīḥ*, 192.

5.4.3.2. Qur'anic Texts as the Completed Result of a Comparison of Religions

Since, in Rayyān's view, the Qur'anic texts contain and express ultimate truth, he seems to consider the prospect of reasoning with Christians unnecessary. Instead, he believes that it is sufficient simply to quote Qur'anic passages in a certain order. According to this understanding, the comparison between true monotheism and false ideas about God, Christ, redemption etc. to have been concluded already. The Qur'anic text contains the result of a comparison that simply has to be accepted and followed.

5.4.3.3. The Qur'anic Text Itself Is the Argument

Rayyān's book does not bother with engaging in reasoning or arguing with Christians. One therefore finds only a few passages that appear offensive. Rather, the book of Rayyān intends merely to state what is true or false, right or wrong. The text of the Qur'an serves as the basis and argument of this procedure. This text is not questioned and does not need to be questioned in any way. Rayyān regards the Qur'an as self-evident. For this reason, he does not even address the historical circumstances of the revelation (*tanzīl* in Arabic) of different passages.

5.4.3.4. Two Truth Criteria

Even though he shows almost no interest in Christian scriptures, history, teachings, and traditions, Rayyān nevertheless addresses Christians with his book. He expects Christians to consider the texts of the Qur'an. His goal is for Christian readers to embrace Islam. It is they who are called upon to compare their beliefs and praxis with the Qur'an. Rayyān therefore operates with two truth criteria: One the one hand, human reason, which has been given to all humans by God, the creator; and, on the other hand, the Qur'an, a text in absolute accordance with human reasoning.

5.5. Rayyān's Approach over against That of Ḥimāiyah – Comparing Comparisons

Thus far, we have considered two Islamic authors, Ḥimāiyah and Rayyān. Whereas Ḥimāiyah's approach to the comparison of religions is evident, Rayyān's way of doing comparison remains rather implicit. Let us now summarize the similarities and differences between the two approaches.

5.5.1. Similarities

5.5.1.1. Human Reason and the Reasonable Message of the Qur'an

Both authors presuppose that God as the creator of all beings has provided human beings with reason. Since it is assumed that the revelation of God as given in the

Qur'an is also reasonable, human beings have a natural tendency, then, to trust in the message of the Qur'an and to adhere to its commands. Therefore the pursuit of a comparison of religions is aimed at communicating the reasonable content of the Qur'an, either by arguing or by simply repeating Qur'anic texts.

5.5.1.2. Qur'anic Texts as Self-evident Proof of Truth

Because of its very nature, both authors regard the Qur'anic text as self-evident. Neither gives any information about when and where particular passages were revealed, about the original addressees, or about the historical circumstances. Whereas Islamic exegesis is concerned with the *asbāb an-nuzūl* in order better to understand the meaning of the Qur'anic text, both authors deem this procedure to be irrelevant, at least as far as Christian opponents and their false teachings are concerned. The Qur'anic texts are regarded as providing the eternal truth about these matters, that is, the oneness of God (*tawḥīd* in Arabic) and other teachings.

5.5.1.3. The Christian Counterpart Interpreted from an Islamic Perspective

Both authors are concerned only with "Christians" as depicted in the Qur'an. Therefore, their considerations are done entirely from an Islamic perspective. The comparison of religions cannot reveal new insights because the Qur'an has already spoken the final word about the false teachings of Christians. Such a comparison therefore simply amounts to a correction of the Other, instead of learning from or even arguing with her.

5.5.1.4. Ignoring the Other's Self-understanding

This kind of comparison is not really concerned with the self-understanding of the Other. The inner logic of Christian thought does not factor into the consideration. The results of Christian theological thinking or exegesis are not taken into account. Whereas Ḥimāiyah at least references a few brief quotations from very old Christian sources, Rayyān does not refer to any Christian sources at all.

5.5.2. Differences

5.5.2.1. Comparing Texts as Opposed to Proclaiming "the" Text

Beside the similarities, there are some profound differences between Ḥimāiyah's approach and that of Rayyān. Ḥimāiyah's approach aims to convince the reader by comparing Qur'anic texts with Biblical texts. Even though the quotations are not very long, the author tries to show that New Testament texts contradict either themselves or human reasoning. By comparing different texts from both sides, the author argues against the backdrop of a certain kind of metaphysical logic.

In contrast, Rayyān refrains from such argumentation. His style is less aggressive and offensive, and more affirmative: Since the Qur'anic texts reveal ultimate truth, any kind of human reasoning is deemed obsolete. It suffices simply to let the Qur'anic texts speak for themselves. Even though these texts are regarded as self-evident, the author arranges them in a particular order to show a stringent line of thought.

5.5.2.2. Using Christian Sources as Opposed to Avoiding Christian Texts

Ḥimāiyah in his book regularly points to and quotes Biblical texts, whereas Rayyān refers only to the New Testament in general. Whereas Ḥimāiyah also uses material from the Ḥadīth tradition and points to Muslim thinkers like Riḍa and others, Rayyān sticks almost entirely to Qur'anic texts. Even so, neither author is interested in explaining Qur'anic texts or Christian texts according to their context or historical circumstances. The mere quotation of the Qur'an is deemed to be sufficient.

5.5.2.3. Ridiculing the Other as Opposed to Informing the Other

The argumentative style of Ḥimāiyah sometimes amounts to an aggressive and polemical apologetic tone. Rayyān refrains from using such a tone. Instead, he simply states that the theological ideas and issues he presents are the truth. He leaves the judgment and comparison to the readers. Even though Ḥimāiyah claims to argue in the best and most neutral manner, he often ridicules Christian teachings, at least the way he understands them. Rayyān does not proceed in this manner.

5.6. Conclusion

The approaches of Ḥimāiyah and Rayyān are similar in some ways, but they also show some striking differences when it comes to the method applied. The next chapter will deal with a third thinker named Ahmad Shalabi. After describing Shalabi's approach to the comparison of religions, all three thinkers will need to be compared with regard to methodology. As will be shown, we can discern three different approaches to the "comparison of religions," even though we will need to ask whether the label "comparison of religions" is justified in each case by the standards of Western scholarship.

6. Ahmad Shalabi (1915-2000)

Having compared two scholars of al-Azhar University in terms of their approaches to the comparison of religions, it may be useful to add a third voice. Ahmad Shalabi is a well-known writer in Egypt. He taught at al-Azhar for a period of time, but not for his whole life. Nevertheless, his approach to the comparison of religions is worth studying, since his books are available in many bookstores in the country.

6.1. Biographical Notes

Ahmad Shalabi was born in Sharkiyya-City in northeastern Egypt in 1915. In his early years, he studied at an al-Azhar elementary school (*kuttāb* in Arabic). There he managed to memorize the Qur'an under the tutelage of a sheikh. He continued his schooling at al-Azhar high school. He also received tertiary education, graduating from *Dār al-'Ulūm* in Cairo in 1945 with a diploma in education and psychology. Later on, he studied in the United Kingdom as well, earning a Master's Degree from the University of London and a Doctoral Degree from Cambridge University. From 1955 until 1961, he worked as the Director of the Egyptian Cultural Center in Indonesia. After returning to Egypt, he worked as an assistant professor at *Dār al-'Ulūm*, which by then had been incorporated into Cairo University. He headed the department of *Islamic History and Civilization* (*tarīḫ al-islāmī wa al-ḥadara* in Arabic). Shalabi also worked as a guest lecturer at different universities in Pakistan, Malaysia, and Indonesia. Later on, he became a member of the Egyptian Supreme Council of Culture and also a member of UNESCO. He published a number of books in Arabic, English, and Indonesian. In addition, he also featured in several TV and radio programs. He became director of the journal of Islamic studies named *al-Zahrā'* (*the clarity* or *flower* in Arabic). This journal is published by the *Islamic Studies Association*. In 1987, he was awarded the Order of the Republic of Egypt. Shalabi died in 2000.

6.2. Shalabi's Book *Al-Masīḥīya – Muqāranat al-Adyan*, Vol. 2

Shalabi wrote a series of four volumes on the "comparison of religions" (*muqāranat al-adyan* in Arabic). Volume 1 was dedicated to the Jewish religion (*al-yahudiyya* in Arabic), volume 2 to the Christian religion (*al-masiḥiyya* in Arabic), volume 3 to Islam (*al-islām* in Arabic), and volume 4 to Indian religions (*al-adyan al India al-qubra* in Arabic). We will proceed by giving, firstly, an overview of the content, secondly, some observations on Shalabi's methodology, thirdly, an analysis of the Christian and Muslim sources he uses, and, fourthly, an outline of his main ideas about Christianity. The first edition of Shalabi's book *al-Masīḥīya – Muqāranat al-Adyan, Vol. 2* appeared in 1984. Currently, the eighth edition is available, printed in 2018.[1] – After distilling Shalabi's approach to the "comparison of religions" in chapter 6 of our study, we will go on in chapter 7 to compare Shalabi's approach to those of Maḥmūd Ḥimāiyah and Taha Rayyān.

6.2.1. Content

For ease of reference, we will provide the page numbers for the parts of Shalabi's book in brackets following the description. After the *Introduction of the Publisher* (p. 5), Shalabi provides his own *Introduction to the Eighth Edition* (pp. 7-9). He then proceeds with a *General Introduction* (pp. 11-21), followed by the first chapter, entitled *Summary of the Journey of Christianity* (pp. 22-26).

The title of the second chapter is *The Most Famous Approaches to Christ and Christianity* (pp. 27-87). This chapter is divided into three subchapters. Firstly, *Christ and Christianity According to Muslims* (pp. 27-69), secondly, *Christ and Christianity according to Western Thinkers* (pp. 69-80), and, thirdly, *Christ and Christianity according to Christians* (pp. 80-87). The first subchapter is dedicated almost entirely to the Qur'an according to the interpretation of the author and other scholars, as well as to quotations from the gospels. The second subchapter focuses on the views of a number of Western thinkers on Christianity.

Chapter 3 is entitled *The Current Christianity and Its Founder* (*al-masiḥīya wa-wāḍ'hā* in Arabic) (pp. 88-104), followed by chapter 4 on *The Translatability of Christianity According to Present-day Christians* (*tafṣīl al-qaul 'an al-masiḥīya 'inda al-masiḥīīna al-ān* in Arabic) (pp. 105-141). The subchapters of chapter 4 read as follows: *The Trinity in Christianity* (pp. 105-117); *The Divinity of Christ and the Council of Nicea* (pp. 117-125); *The Divinity of the Holy Spirit* (pp. 125-127); *The Crucifixion of Christ for the Atonement of Human Sin* (pp. 127-134); *Christ Judges Human Beings* (pp. 135-137); and *Christian Praxis* (137-141), referring to Baptism and the Lord's Supper. After a broad overview of Christian thinkers and comments on specific Christian doctrines, Shalabi proceeds with chapters on a number of different topics: *The True Sources of Christian Doctrine* (pp. 141-154); *The Nature of Christ and Opinions about It* (pp. 155-166); *The Bible* (166-186); *Legislation (to Institute Sharia) and Christianity* (pp. 187-194); *The Most Famous Christian Denominations Today* (pp. 194-199); *The Church and its Practices and Secrets* (pp. 200-208); *The Religious Reformation Movement* (pp. 209-217); *Christianity according to Scholarly Criticism* (pp. 218-230); *The Matter of Divinity – An Example for Comparison between Religious Issues* (pp. 231-248); and, finally, the *Bibliography* (pp. 249-252).

[1] Ahmad Shalabi, *Al-Masīḥīya – Muqāranat al-Adyan*, vol. 2, 8th ed. (Cairo: Dār al-Ma'ārif, 2018).

The table of contents reveals a certain order of thinking, but not a very systematic approach. We now have to address the methodology used by the author, before we proceed to analyze the sources to which he refers.

6.2.2. The Introduction of the Book – References to Methodology

In order to describe Shalabi's approach to the comparison of religions, one has to pay attention not only to the semantics, but also to the semiotics of the book, as well as to the information given in the introductory section.

6.2.2.1. The Comparison of Religions as a Religious Undertaking

Concerning the semiotics of the book, it is important to observe that in the introduction, Shalabi cites Surah 29:46 of the Qur'an: "Argue only in the best way with the People of the Book, except with those of them who act unjustly. Say, 'We believe in what was revealed to us and in what was revealed to you; our God and your God are one [and the same]; we are devoted to Him.'"

Prefacing the book with this quotation signals that the author intends to provide arguments regarding the understanding between Muslims and Christians. With regard to the comparison of religions, this suggests that the author is not interested in merely describing differences between the two religions, but that he is more interested in arguing about the truth claims of the two religions. Therefore, the reader should expect the author to deal with the question of religious truth, meaning that the comparison of religions is understood as a religious undertaking.

6.2.2.2. Following the Example of the Prophet Muḥammad

In the introduction to the 8th edition, Shalabi begins by mentioning that he is grateful to have had the opportunity to teach courses on the comparison of religions at different universities worldwide and recently also at al-Azhar University's *Faculty of Sharia and Law* (*sharia* and *kanūn* in Arabic). He also mentions that his books have begun to be translated into different languages.[2] Shalabi states that after the release of the first edition in 1984, he received a number of reactions from the Christian side, with some responding positively, others opposing his understanding of Christianity.[3]

Then he tells the story of how he was invited by members of a Rotary Club in Cairo, a number of whom were Christians. He explains that he accepted the invitation according to the example of the prophet Muḥammad, who talked to a delegation of Christians from Najrān. With regard to this example, the author quotes the well-known *ayat* from Surah al-Imran (Surah 3:64): "Say, 'People of the Book, let us arrive at a statement that is common to us all [or: a common word]: we worship God alone, we ascribe no partner to Him, and none of us takes others

[2] Shalabi, *Al-Masīḥīya*, 7.
[3] Shalabi, *Al-Masīḥīya*, 8.

besides God as lords.' If they turn away, say, 'Witness our devotion to Him.'" Shalabi states that he quoted this verse when answering a question raised by a Christian participant at the meeting.[4] This Christian had asked the author's opinion about conflicts between Muslims and Christians. Shalabi claims that this *ayat* from Surah al-Imran is the most important Islamic text with regard to Muslim-Christian relations. He goes on to state that all religions stem from one and the same source. He holds to the metaphor that all religions are like the links of a chain: If one link were lacking, the reader would miss something very important.

These examples show that the author understands his work as a contribution to the clarification of Islamic positions and of an Islamic understanding of the religious Other. As part of the introduction to the eighth edition, these examples have to do with the political situation in recent years. In order to get a better understanding of the operative methodology used in the comparison of religions here, we have to analyze now the general introduction.

6.2.2.3. Comparison of Religions as an Effort along the Way of God (jihād)

The general introduction begins with a prayer. The author states that writing this book is part of his *jihād*, just as others do their *jihād* with a sword, money, or other means. He asks God to accept his (Shalabi's) effort (*jihād* in Arabic).[5]

After the prayer, he proceeds by claiming that Christianity is the most complicated of all religions. Although 'Īsā taught a simple and easy religion, later on, more and more complications appeared. The understanding of Christianity and its doctrine became more and more complex. In claiming this the author refers to Roland Benton.[6] In a biographical note, Shalabi explains that when he gave lectures on the comparison of religions in Indonesia, he observed that Christian mission was becoming stronger and was spreading fast. For this reason, he felt obliged to allow his lectures to be published in other languages as a reaction to Christian efforts.[7] This explanation shows that the author understands his way of doing comparison of religions to be related to the rivalry between Muslims and Christians.

In another example, he tells the story of an interreligious debate in which he took part. The reaction of the audience – according to the author – was positive, not because of his person, but because of their knowledge of the Islamic religion. He states that on this occasion, the answers of Christians to his questions were weak and not scholarly at all.[8] After concluding the example, the author emphasizes: "This book is not a response to the books that attack Islam."[9]

[4] Shalabi, *Al-Masīḥīya*, 9.
[5] Shalabi, *Al-Masīḥīya*, 11.
[6] Shalabi, *Al-Masīḥīya*, 12.
[7] Shalabi, *Al-Masīḥīya*, 12.
[8] Shalabi, *Al-Masīḥīya*, 13.
[9] Shalabi, *Al-Masīḥīya*, 15.

6.2.2.4. Comparison of Religions in the Context of Christian-Muslim Competition

At this point, it is interesting to note that the author is still speaking of a book that is supposed to deal entirely with Christianity, not with Islam. In his introduction, the author nevertheless talks about books that have insulted Islam and the Qur'an. He claims not to react against these books. Rather, he states that he intends to portray Christianity according to its original sources. This approach, he says, will lead to a portrayal or description of Christianity that is close to perfection. The author states: "This book... helped to convert millions of people and saved them from Christian mission. I lived in Asia for several years, and I saw Christian mission spreading rapidly all over Asia, trying to attract millions of people to Christianity."[10] This passage shows the intention of the author to compete with what he claims to be Christian efforts of evangelization. The framework of the author therefore is the *call to Islam* (*da'wah*). This Christianity the author claims to be a political Christianity which – according to him – is not in line with the Christianity of 'Īsā.[11] Shalabi laments that Christian mission is carried out by missionaries, diplomats, new books, journals, radio, hospitals, schools, and training of foreign youth in European countries. He continues by speaking about Christian mission in majority Muslim countries. This – according to the author – requires an Islamic response, which he is willing to provide in this book.[12] The eighth edition, the author explains, has been expanded with new material and new references, just as the previous editions had been expanded as well.

6.2.2.5. References to Shalabi's Methodology

With regard to Shalabi's methodology in this book, one may summarize as follows: (1) He intends to pursue an approach that does not address interreligious conflicts. (2) Nevertheless, the author clearly formulates his deliberations within the framework of Christian-Muslim competition. (3) Shalabi claims that methodologically, he will follow the example of the Qur'an and the prophet Muḥammad. (4) In order to describe Christianity, the author refrains from dealing only with Islamic sources (especially the Qur'an), but claims to make use of original Christian sources as well. (5) This may raise the expectation that the author's intention is to understand Christianity on the basis of its own framework of thought. Whether the author achieves this goal or not is a question that will need to be asked after the completion of our analysis.

6.2.2.6. Christian and Muslim Sources

Shalabi writes that his most important source for understanding Christianity is the Bible itself. In addition, he mentions a book in the Indonesian language published

---

[10] Shalabi, *Al-Masīḥīya*, 16.

[11] Shalabi, *Al-Masīḥīya*, 17.

[12] Shalabi, *Al-Masīḥīya*, 17-18.

and used by the Roman Catholic Church.[13] In terms of Western scholars, he mentions such books as Gerald L. Berry's *Religions of the World*; Adolf von Harnack's *What is Christianity*; William Patoun's *Great Religions of the World*; the *Encyclopedia of Religions and Ethics*; the *Encyclopedia Britannica*; and Wells' *A Short History of the World*.[14]

With regard to sources in the Arabic language, Shalabi states that he used books by Christian authors such as Al-Qiss Bulus Sabāt, Al-Qiss Ibrahim Said, Al-Qiss Butar, and Habib Said.[15] Besides those, he also used books by Islamic authors such as Muḥammad 'Abduh and Muḥammad Abū Zahra.[16]

The selection of sources shows that the author does not refer to theologians like Augustine, Thomas Aquinas, Martin Luther, or Karl Barth. Instead, he points to books like that of Berry. Berry's book deals with Christianity on but a few pages. Throughout the book, Berry not demonstrate a deep understanding of Christian doctrine and Christian theology. What then are the main points of Shalabi's understanding of Christianity?

6.3. Christianity and Christians according to Shalabi

Shalabi argues that the apostle Paul and not 'Īsā should be regarded as the founder of Christianity as a religion. According to Shalabi, Paul added a number of teachings to those of 'Īsā. Shalabi therefore distinguishes between the "Religion of Paul" and the "Religion of 'Īsā." He states: "'Īsā was Jewish till the end, but Saul who later called himself Paul was actually the founder of Christianity. What made him distinct were his innovation and knowledge of politics, while 'Īsā received dreams and illusions."[17] What then are the characteristics of what Shalabi calls "the Religion of Paul"?

6.3.1. The Religion of 'Īsā and the Religion of Paul

The author states that the religion of 'Īsā disappeared in the 40s and 50s of the first century. It was replaced by the religion of Paul:

> In this regard, witness the fourth and fifth decade after the Christian birth of 'Īsā. [His religion] withers, some of its positions change, while others disappear. His followers are scattered to the winds. These two decades also see the religion of Paul emerging in the name of Christianity.[18]

The author calls this a "shift" (*taḥūl* in Arabic).

---

[13] Shalabi, *Al-Masīḥīya*, 14.
[14] Shalabi, *Al-Masīḥīya*, 14.
[15] Shalabi, *Al-Masīḥīya*, 14.
[16] Shalabi, *Al-Masīḥīya*, 15.
[17] Shalabi, *Al-Masīḥīya*, 73.
[18] Shalabi, *Al-Masīḥīya*, 94.

6.3.2. The Religion of Paul – Christianity

Which line of argument does the author employ? Shalabi attempts to demonstrate that a religion called "Christianity" was invented by Paul after the religion of 'Īsā and the real Christians vanished. His hypothesis is that the religion of Paul replaced the religion of 'Īsā. But how could Paul achieve this and why did he convert to Christianity after having opposed and even persecuted Christians?

6.3.2.1. Paul's Authority

Shalabi asserts that Paul never had any direct contact with Jesus Christ. He quotes Gal. 1:11-12 as proof for his assertion that Paul claimed to have received a revelation directly from Christ. This gave him an authority that could not be questioned. "So Saul, who became Paul after he joined Christianity, took the reins in his hand. He never saw Christ or heard him speak, but he claimed a direct connection between himself and Christ, a link which was introduced into Christianity and through which new teachings were given."[19] Shalabi concludes that since Paul claimed to have received this kind of a revelation, he was able to reject every criticism of his teachings.

6.3.2.2. Characteristics of Paul's Religion

According to Shalabi, Paul as the founder of the religion called Christianity introduced a number of new ideas:

> Here are some of the important points that were the foundation of Paul's religion...: 1. Christianity is not only a religion of Israel but a universal religion; 2. Triangulation [of God] through the divinity of Christ and the divinity of the Holy Spirit; 3. The fact that Jesus is the Son of God and comes down to sacrifice himself to atone for the sin of mankind. 4. The resurrection of Jesus from the dead and his ascension to the right hand of his Father, where he was before, to judge and sentence humankind. Perhaps the first point – the fact that Christianity became a universal religion – was the turning point in the history of this religion. Without a doubt, Paul was the first to speak of the universality of Christianity.[20]

The author assumes that Paul purposefully introduced certain elements from different religious traditions in order to attract a broad variety of people:

> In fact the founder of Christianity, Paul, introduced into his religion some of the teachings of the Jews in order to attract the Jewish public, as well as images from the philosophy of the Greeks in order to attract Greek followers, and he began to proclaim that Jesus is Savior and Lord.[21]

---

[19] Shalabi, *Al-Masīḥīya*, 90.

[20] Shalabi, *Al-Masīḥīya*, 92-93.

[21] Shalabi, *Al-Masīḥīya*, 92.

6.3.2.3. Paul's Disciples – Luke and John

Shalabi argues that Paul had a number of disciples, the most influential of whom were Luke and John:

> As previously mentioned, Paul's good student, Luke, teamed up with Paul. There are three epistles that have to do with Paul experiencing similar kinds of attacks by people who opposed him and his ideas. These epistles were mostly talking about John, although they were not written by John. This suspicion may be confirmed when we thoroughly study the style and main concepts of these epistles and then compare them to Paul's style and his thoughts. This study leads me to say that Paul's epistles and the epistles attributed to John actually came from the same source. Hence, I ask the reader to read these epistles carefully. Most readers will reach the same conclusion. Be that as it may, if the assumption is true, then these epistles can be traced back to Paul. And if not, then John followed the progression of Paul's thoughts, as did Luke.[22]

It should be noted that the author at this point asks the reader to compare the letters of Paul with the letters of John in order to prove that a number of ideas, such as Christ being the son of God, are found in both. The comparison is not intended to be a thorough exploration of the theological profile of one of these letters; it is simply intended to classify a number of scriptures and label them as having been corrupted.

6.3.2.4. Conflict between the True Christians and Paul

The author then enquires about the true Christians, the followers of the religion of 'Īsā, as opposed to those adhering to the innovations introduced by Paul:

> *What is the position of the apostles and the true followers of Jesus with regard to Paul's thoughts?* The answer is that a great struggle took place between Paul and his followers, on the one hand, and the true Christians, on the other. The extent of this conflict was great.[23]

One may note that according to Christian scholarship, there have been a number of theological opinions and theological conflicts within the movement called early Christianity. Yet the author does not reference any such scholarship. Instead, he simply posits an opposition between the followers of the religion of 'Īsā and the followers of the religion of Paul. We will need to return to this issue later on.

---

[22] Shalabi, *Al-Masīḥīya*, 98.
[23] Shalabi, *Al-Masīḥīya*, 95.

6.3.2.5. Corruption of the Scriptures

It has already been mentioned that according to Shalabi, Paul had two important disciples, Luke and John. This would imply that the writings of Luke and John were influenced by Paul and the ideas he introduced into Christianity. Bearing in mind that the New Testament is comprised of twenty-seven scriptures, that fourteen of these are generally attributed to Paul, while three letters are attributed to John and one gospel and the book of Acts are attributed to Luke, the author in fact argues that a significant total of nineteen New Testament scriptures were influenced by Paul and therefore have to be regarded as corrupted.[24]

6.3.2.6. The True Christians

Shalabi goes on to ask how the true Christians reacted to the introduction of false teachings by Paul, John, and Luke. He claims that no original scriptures, i.e. scriptures related to the religion of ʿĪsā, still exist. These scriptures have disappeared. If the true religion of ʿĪsā has disappeared, do the corrupted scriptures written by Paul, Luke, and John at least give some hints about this religion? Shalabi answers that some passages of these corrupted scriptures contain stark opposition to certain teachings. These particular passages give a glimpse of the original religion of ʿĪsā, the author claims. He writes:

> *What was the attitude of the real Christians? What was the law or "instruction" that Paul and John warned about? What did they, of whom John said that they ignore the son and his divinity, actually write? Is it possible that none of them wrote anything, that they did not express their opinions, did not defend their beliefs?* The answer is certainly and without any doubt that they did write, or speak, or struggle. That is very clear from John and Paul. But where are their writings, speeches, explanations, and attempts to defend their beliefs? The answer is that we have nothing. It must all have been destroyed by the tyrants in the dark ages, just as they destroyed the gospel of Jesus; perhaps you may say that some of their writings were not destroyed and were hidden by these fellows and then inherited by their children and grandchildren.[25]

6.3.2.7. The Epistle of James and the Gospel of Barnabas

Shalabi believes that only a few New Testament texts are less corrupted than most, like the epistle of James and the Gospel of Matthew. Most of the scriptures of the religion of ʿĪsā were lost. Only one scripture from this religion has been found:

> Those who claimed that Christ was divine picked out what was not against their position in the gospels and early epistles. Also, they

[24] Shalabi, *Al-Masīḥīya*, 96-97.
[25] Shalabi, *Al-Masīḥīya*, 99.

hid or destroyed other scriptures, as we will see when talking about the Holy Book. Only Barnabas' Gospel appeared in the 18th century and survived their attempts of destruction.[26]

6.3.2.8. Why Did Paul Join Christianity?

According to Shalabi, the question remains why Paul, after having persecuted Christians for a long time, finally joined Christianity himself. His answer is that Paul never stopped opposing the religion of 'Īsā, but that he became part of Christianity in order to destroy it. In making this statement, Shalabi presupposes that Paul still had the intention to destroy Christianity when writing his letters. He argues:

> After this brief, comprehensive study, we ask ourselves an important question: What did Paul want from Christianity? Using Christianity, Paul brought about momentous events: their conversion from an Israelite religion to a universal religion; their transfer from monotheism to tripartism; he proclaimed the divinity of Christ and the divinity of the Holy Spirit; he invented the story of redemption for atonement for the sins of mankind; and he abolished aspects established by Jesus himself, such as circumcision and not eating pork. In a word, he created a new religion, as has already been said, appropriating the name Christianity and applying it to himself, thereby obliterating the true Christian religion. Why do all of that? What did Paul want from Christianity?
>
> Many scholars believe that Paul's enmity toward Christianity led him to pretend to join it in order to continue his war using a new weapon, the weapon of destruction from the inside by corrupting its features and obliterating its manifestations and dates.[27]

We may observe that in making these allegations, the author subscribes to a kind of conspiracy theory: Paul conspired against the religion of 'Īsā, became a member of the movement, altered its content, argued against real Christians, and succeeded in establishing a new religion, his own religion, thereby replacing the religion of 'Īsā. The author at this point refers to "many scholars" backing up his claims, but, as so often, gives no names or sources.

6.4. Understanding of the New Testament

The author comes to the conclusion that the twenty-seven scriptures of the New Testament must have been corrupted in different ways, with some scriptures being lost, others being altered, and yet other scriptures being fabricated.

[26] Shalabi, *Al-Masīḥīya*, 100.

[27] Shalabi, *Al-Masīḥīya*, 103-104.

6.4.1. Lost Scriptures

According to Shalabi, the religion of ‘Īsā came to an end as a result of persecution and oppression. After a certain time, the religion of Paul replaced the religion of ‘Īsā. The religion of Paul, according to the author, was favored by the Roman empire:

> A period of time passed after Jesus’ principles and apostles passed away and their cultural heritage was lost or disappeared. Paul’s thoughts dominated, particularly when the Roman power supported this trend and combated any other trend. But the truth did not disappear completely. It struggled on from one age to another. Indeed, the truth shall prevail and triumph at the end.[28]

This passage shows that the author expects the “truth” to triumph, by which he means the truth of the true religion of ‘Īsā. One may ask how Shalabi can know about this true religion of ‘Īsā, if not from the Christian sources? The answer is that he presupposes the Islamic understanding of the religion of ‘Īsā. We will have to revisit this question later.

6.4.2. Scriptures of Which the Contents Have Been Altered

While the scriptures of the religion of ‘Īsā were lost, some of the existing scriptures of the New Testament may have been altered, the author claims:

> 1. Gospels and writings that opposed Paul vanished forever, including Jesus’ gospel and what the apostles wrote, as previously mentioned. 2. Those that did not oppose the ideas of Paul, such as the Gospel of Matthew and the Gospel of Mark, were saved from being handed over to destruction – but that does not exclude the possibility that some changes may have been made by Paul’s supporters, such as leaving some things out or adding others, especially in the process of translating them from Aramaic into the languages of the nations which Paul called to Christianity.[29]

Here Shalabi simply assumes that there had been an Aramaic version of the Gospel of Matthew and the Gospel of Mark. He assumes three different kinds of alteration or distortion: Firstly, alteration via translation into a different language; secondly, the introduction of new passages; and, thirdly, the deletion of passages. One may observe that the author uses this argument to apply the Islamic teaching of distortion (*taḥrīf* in Arabic) to the New Testament.

[28] Shalabi, *Al-Masīḥīya*, 100.
[29] Shalabi, *Al-Masīḥīya*, 101.

6.4.3. Scriptures with Fabricated Contents

Shalabi alleges that a number of New Testament scriptures were corrupted even more than others. All the scriptures written by disciples of Paul are regarded as highly distorted:

> 3. The Gospel of Luke, the Gospel of John, and the epistles are all Paulish. They are attributed without doubt to Paul and his followers, and if we recall what we mentioned above about the full cooperation between Paul, Luke, and John, then we realize that the vast majority of these sources were the works of Paul and his disciples, such as the Gospel of Luke and the Gospel of John. There are fourteen letters which are the handiwork of Paul, and three by John. There is the Revelation of John and the letter of the Acts of the Apostles, which was written by Luke. As a result, the greater part – if not all – of the sources of Christianity have strong ties to Paul's pen and imagination or were manufactured by his followers.[30]

6.4.4. A Scripture That Is Less Distorted

What surprises Shalabi is that at least one scripture of the true Christians survived the destruction. Here he is speaking about the letter of James, because this particular letter contains a number of teachings not rejected by the author. To Shalabi, this indicates that the letter of Jacob mirrors some of the characteristics of the religion of ʻĪsā, the religion of the true Christians:

> 3. What remains from these sources is the important missive written by James. It alone is a model, and it is amazing that it escaped destruction and was able to keep its place in the New Testament. Whoever reads this letter realizes that he is being confronted by a new style and new ideas. Neither does [James] speak of the divinity of Christ, nor of him having come down to offer himself for the redemption of human sin, nor of his rising from the dead and sitting down on the right hand of his Father. And [James] does not appeal to "other Christians," but presents a quiet sermon and examples that are easy to understand, without any embellishment or alteration.[31]

6.5. The Divinity of Christ and the Trinity

As has been shown above, Shalabi bases his argumentation on a certain understanding of the history of early Christianity. The emphasis lies in particular on the phenomena of persecution und the use of force.

---

[30] Shalabi, *Al-Masīḥīya*, 101.

[31] Shalabi, *Al-Masīḥīya*, 101.

6.5.1. History of the Early Church

The author claims that Christianity was persecuted for three centuries. This claim serves as an argument for the thesis that not only were a large number of "true" Christians (according to the author's definition) killed, but the original texts were also destroyed. Secondly, the author argues that the decisions of the church council in the year 325 had been influenced by the Roman emperor.[32] Yet it must be noted that the historical remarks of the author are superficial in the sense that there is no attempt to deal with the theological issues at stake. The decision of 325, in the author's view, clearly went against monotheism.[33]

6.5.2. Influences of Greek Philosophy and Ancient Religions

The author traces the ideas of the Trinity and of Christ being the son of God back to Greek philosophy and to ancient religions like the cult of Osiris,[34] among others. In so doing, Shalabi gives no references to back up his claims. Instead, he points to the books authored by Wells and Berry. Shalabi himself does not discuss the theological concepts of early Christianity. He only provides some four or five references from the New Testament.

6.5.3. Biblical References

According to the author, one may quote Matt. 3:17, John 1:1, 3, 14, or Matt. 26:26 as proof that Jesus is called the son of God. Instead of interpreting these texts within the framework of the scripture in question, Shalabi quotes Western thinkers in order to show that the idea of the divinity of Christ is of foreign origin.[35] Concerning the Gospel of John, he claims that this scripture was written long after the time of Jesus. Therefore, he argues, the connection to Jesus was lost. By quoting references where Jesus is called to be a prophet, the author alleges that Jesus was nothing but a human being and a messenger.

6.6. Shalabi's Method of Comparison of Religions

One may ask whether the method of Shalabi actually deserves to be called a comparison of religions. After all, what does he compare? It has become obvious that Shalabi compares the true religion of 'Īsā with the religion of Paul. He argues historically that Paul invented Christianity by purposefully introducing pagan ideas to it, after first having tried to destroy the religion of 'Īsā by force. Shalabi's historical claims are thus based on a conspiracy theory. His argumentation is clearly apologetic. Nevertheless, we have to ask what kind of methodology he uses.

---

[32] Shalabi, *Al-Masīḥīya*, 117-125.

[33] Shalabi, *Al-Masīḥīya*, 118ff.

[34] Shalabi, *Al Masīḥīya*, 118.

[35] Shalabi, *Al-Masīḥīya*, 121-123.

6.6.1. Shalabi's Usage of Christian Sources

It is noteworthy that Shalabi uses only a handful of books by Westerners. Most of these books deal with religions in a rather superficial way, since these books are simply overviews of different religions. Furthermore, these books are old, having been written in the 19th century or at the beginning of the 20th century. Not a single book of well-known modern-day Christian theologians is cited, nor a single book on exegesis. The author is not proficient in ancient Hebrew, ancient Greek, or Latin.

Shalabi quotes his sources only to support his ideas about Christian history. There is not a single instance where he uses any of his sources in order to represent or engage with a critical voice dissenting from his opinion. Furthermore, the quotations are very short, where quotations are given at all. In a number of passages, the author makes a claim and says that philosophers or certain thinkers support his ideas – but he provides no references to warrant his claims.

With regard to New Testament texts, Shalabi uses quotations in an attempt to prove his ideas. To give only one example: The author claims that there was a struggle between real Christians, i.e. followers of the religion of ʻĪsā, and followers of Paul, that is, people who proclaimed the religion of Paul named Christianity. In order to prove that there was such a struggle, he cherry-picks quotations from different letters of the New Testament without giving any references to the scriptural context of the quotations as part of a broader text. The quotations are stripped entirely of their contexts.

It is legitimate to ask what kind of a "comparison" this is. Apparently, this is a comparison arising from Shalabi's Islamic belief that there once existed a religion of ʻĪsā that must have been in line with Islamic teachings and especially with the message of the Qur'an. Shalabi then searches for this kind of religion within the body of New Testament scriptures. His intention then is not to understand these scriptures on the basis of their own context. A theology of Matthew, Mark, or John is not relevant for him, since according to his understanding, these scriptures are to be labeled as distorted.

On this point there is a similarity between Ḥimāiyah and Shalabi. The difference lies in the line of argument. Ḥimāiyah, by using quotations from the New Testament, tries to show that Christian teachings are false, illogical, and foolish. For this reason, he searches for what he believes to be inconsistencies, errors, or fairytales. Shalabi would probably agree with this idea, but his intention is different. Instead of arguing that the texts contradict each other and generally contradict human reasoning, Shalabi intends to show that the New Testament scriptures are highly distorted. His argument is that one can find within these texts hints that point to the real history of early Christianity. According to Shalabi's conspiracy theory, it was Paul who hated the religion of ʻĪsā and therefore joined the fold of Christians in order to destroy the movement from within by introducing false teachings, rites, and regulations.

Both authors, Ḥimāiyah and Shalabi, intend to undermine the credibility of the New Testament scriptures. While Ḥimāiyah uses quotations from the New Testament to prove the alleged corruption by showing inconsistency between the quoted passages, Shalabi uses quotations to prove the history of early Christianity as a history of corruption and distortion. Both authors contend that the original Christian scriptures were lost; both highlight the theory of *taḥrīf*. While Ḥimāiyah is polemical in tone, Shalabi is less offensive, but nonetheless clear in his rejection of the New Testament scriptures, except for the epistle of James.

6.6.2. Use of Muslim Sources

Shalabi rarely makes use of any Muslim sources, that is, he seldomly quotes passages from the Qur'an or by Muslim thinkers. He confines himself to making claims about the allegedly "true" history of Christianity. Neverthelees, it has to be noted that the theory of "Paul as a Jewish deceiver – a pseudo-convert to Christianity whose sole intention is to deceive Christians and corrupt their faith" is rather old, for it is already to found among writers like Sayf ibn ᶜUmar al-Tamīmī (d. 796-7) or ᶜAbd al-Jabbār (d. 1025).[36]

[36] Kuhn, Michael F. "Early Islamic Perspectives of the Apostle Paul as a Narrative Framework for Taḥrīf." In *Arab Christians and the Qur'an from the Origins of Islam to the Medieval Period*. Edited by Mark Beaumont. Leiden: Brill, 2018, 153-167. Kuhn states: "ᶜAbd al-Jabbār´s writing is unique among Muslims until his time period in that it provides detail as to when, how and why *taḥrīf* (corruption) took place. In effect, ᶜAbd al-Jabbār seeks to undermine the *tawatur* [historical credibility, FA] of Christian Scriptures." (162)

7. Three Approaches to the Comparison of Religions – A Summary

Having analyzed the approaches of Ḥimāiyah, Rayyān, and Shalabi, it is clear that each of the three has a different take on the comparison of religions. As mentioned, the term "comparison of religions" applies to the work of all three authors only in a very specific sense, since each of them takes for granted that the only yardstick for comparing different religions is – and can only can be – the Qur'anic message. In their view, then, the comparison has effectively been completed already, because the outcome of any attempted comparison is already given in the message of the Qur'an. In this sense, all three approaches can be called apologetic. Nevertheless, there are some major differences between them that we will now summarize. We will differentiate between direct comparison (Ḥimāiyah), indirect comparison (Rayyān), and undermining comparison (Shalabi).

7.1. Direct Comparison: The Apologetic Approach – Ḥimāiyah

By quoting from both Biblical texts and Qur'anic texts, Ḥimāiyah intends to show the reader the weaknesses of the New Testament texts and theological ideas. Therefore, one may speak in his case of a method of direct comparison: Ḥimāiyah takes the reader by the hand and shows him that the New Testament texts must have been corrupted, because all too often, the content of these texts contradicts human reason. By using metaphysical ideas about God like the invisibility of God, Ḥimāiyah claims that the New Testament stories are illogical, since, to give but one example, if Jesus were truly God, he would have to be invisible. But this is obviously not the case.

The method Ḥimāiyah uses is an attempt actively to convince the reader that only the Qur'anic message can be true. This prompts him to use an apologetic and at times even sarcastic tone. This tone contradicts Ḥimāiyah's stated claim of intending to pursue a comparison of religions in the best, i.e. in a non-offensive manner. It also contradicts his claim to take a scholarly approach to the comparison of religions. As shown, even though Ḥimāiyah visited and lived in Western countries for quite some time, he does not demonstrate any profound knowledge of Christian theology, let alone proficiency in languages like ancient Hebrew, ancient

Greek, or Latin. He also does not show any knowledge of the self-interpretation of Christian theology or doctrine.

7.2. Indirect Comparison: The Affirmative Approach – Rayyān

Rayyān operates with a different method. He confines himself to quotations from the Qur'an. He does not engage in arguing, does not quote New Testament texts, and does not speak in an unfriendly manner; he simply affirms the teachings of the Qur'an. Like Ḥimāiyah, Rayyān is convinced that all the information necessary to understand the religion of 'Īsā, who was a Muslim, as well as the religion of Christianity since the days of the ancient church, including its deviations, is given in the Qur'an. Therefore Rayyān does not believe that it is his task to engage in the comparison of religions as such; he simply invites Christians, his addressees, to read his book, a book that contains Qur'anic texts arranged in a certain order.

For Rayyān, the comparison of religions is not done by actively arguing, like Himayah; it is done indirectly by the Christian reader, who, by reading Qur'anic texts, is called upon to compare the content of these texts with what she has heard thus far concerning Christian teachings given in the New Testament and in the Christian doctrine of the ancient church. Therefore we are justifying in calling Rayyān's approach that of indirect comparison, since he leaves the work of comparison to the reader. The yardstick is given in the Qur'anic texts. Since all humans are bestowed with reason, and since the Qur'an does not contradict reason, as the New Testament stories do, the reader will in a sense automatically come to the conclusion that the Qur'an is right and that the New Testament must be wrong and distorted. In his affirmative manner, Rayyān does not need to display aggression or hostility, because he is convinced that the comparison of religions has already been achieved in the Qur'an.

7.3. Undermining Comparison: The Historical Approach – Shalabi

Shalabi's approach is, once again, different. He does not argue by quoting texts from the Bible next to texts from the Qur'an, nor does he confine himself to the Qur'anic message, but he tries to show from a historical perspective that the message of the New Testament is a distorted one. Thus he undermines the credibility of Christian sources by proposing a history based on a conspiracy theory: that the Christian praxis, creed, and scriptures have been corrupted intentionally by Paul, who was an enemy of the religion of 'Īsā. Shalabi's main reasoning is that there is no real need to compare Biblical texts with Qur'anic texts, since the New Testament stories are almost entirely corrupted.

The yardstick for comparison is once again the Qur'anic message, since Shalabi believes that the true religion of 'Īsā, which was lost, can be accessed only through the texts of the Qur'an. Therefore, whatever historical reconstruction is performed must conform with the Qur'anic critique of the understanding of 'Īsā as the son of God, savior of humankind, and redeemer, of the Trinity and so on. In this approach, the Qur'anic message is used as a tool to reconstruct the history of Christianity.

It becomes obvious that the methodology Shalabi proposes conflicts with all manner of scholarly work done by historians worldwide, since it is not an open approach but a fixed idea of what may have taken place. Therefore, the Qur'anic message is made to provide a kind of blueprint of what could be the outcome of historical research. Christian sources and Christian scholarship are therefore not needed nor considered.

7.4. Conclusion and Open Questions

From the perspective of Western scholarship, none of these approaches deserve to be called a true "comparison of religions," since they are all dogmatically constrained by the Qur'anic message and do not even intend to consider Christian or other sources according to their own self-understanding. Nevertheless, Western scholars must take the methods of Ḥimāiyah, Rayyān, and Shalabi seriously for the simple reason that thinkers like these keep on publishing books and gain a great deal of influence among many people. It is the goal of this research to show that these approaches are being used today in the context of the Egyptian academy as typified by al-Azhar University. It becomes obvious how huge the gap is between such apologetical approaches and Western historical-critical scholarship.

It is necessary to take these thinkers into account in order to understand how Muslim readers are often influenced in the way they view and approach Christians and their teachings. These books show why Muslims influenced by the thinking of authors such as Ḥimāiyah, Rayyān, or Shalabi reject the idea of engaging in dialogue with members of other religions in a manner that is open to listen and to learn, since none of these authors show any intention to listen to anything other than the Qur'anic view – as they define it.

These apologetic works, available to scholars of al-Azhar, seem to function as obstacles to dialogue between people of different faiths. Their kind of comparison of religions serves apologetic intentions only. There is not much openness to interreligious dialogue in Egypt today. The following chapters are intended to provide a glimpse of what is going on in Egypt today. Having done so, we will grapple with the issues and make suggestions for a more helpful approach to the comparison of religions to enable us to come to a better mutual understanding.

8. Christian Voices on Muslim-Christian Relations in Egypt 2019 – Interviews

Having scrutinized the work of three Azhari scholars in the field of the comparison of religions, it might be useful to provide some information about the current situation in Egypt, and especially with regard to Christian-Muslim relations following the so-called Arab Spring of 2011 and the rise of the presidency of General as-Sīsi. On March 24 and 28, 2019, I conducted four interviews with representatives of the major institutions of higher theological education of the Coptic Catholic Church, the Coptic Orthodox Church, and the Coptic Evangelical Church. I will proceed by giving a summary of important issues raised in these interviews. Even though this information may be called "anecdotal evidence," it nevertheless provides valuable insights.

8.1. Christian Seminaries

8.1.1. Father Hadiyya – The Coptic Catholic Seminary, Cairo

Father Hadiyya of the *Coptic Catholic Seminary* (*Kulliyat al-Lahūt al-Iklirikiyya al-Katulik bi-l Maady* in Arabic) is a professor of religion.[1] According to Father Hadiyya, the Catholic Church is very engaged in dialogue and in building good relations with Muslims. He stresses that the official teachings of the Roman Catholic Church have to be covered in theological formation, even though his own opinion differs from these teachings in some respects. To him, Christians in Egypt – regardless of the church to which they belong – have a very important obligation to show the majority Muslim society that they too are true Egyptians. Father Hadiyya believes that this is done in three ways: firstly, by expressing Christian love in everyday life; secondly, by way of a broad diaconical engagement to meet the needs of the Egyptian people, especially the poor and disadvantaged people of society; and, thirdly, by organizing seminars in order to discuss social and ethical issues related to Egyptian society.

Speaking about the prospect of theological dialogue between Christians and Muslims, he believes that such dialogue is important, but admits that it would be difficult to realize for a number of reasons. Firstly, most ordinary citizens of Egypt

[1] Father Hadiyya, interview by author, at the Coptic Catholic Seminary in al-Maady, Cairo, March 24, 2019.

are not well-educated; secondly, the public atmosphere is filled with tension, which hinders a free exchange of ideas; thirdly, potential dialogue organizers hesitate to proceed because they fear unexpected consequences; and, fourthly, both sides deal with religion in very personal and inflexible ways, which makes it difficult for both to rethink their own positions.

In terms of his own approach to tackling issues in the field of Christian-Muslim relations, Father Hadiyya employs a twofold strategy, distinguishing between theoretical and practical aspects. Theoretically speaking, he teaches the importance of dialogue and the methodology of dialogue. He stresses the different dimensions of living together in harmony. Practically speaking, he encourages case studies by tasking his students with field research. Their task is to study a specific problem in society and to propose solutions for it.

Asked about the future of Christians in Egypt, he answers that the security of the Christian population is always related to the political situation and especially to the political leadership. Since the presidency of General as-Sīsi, the state has attempted to improve the security situation all over the country. Although everybody benefits from such attempts per se, they would be even more effective if they were coupled with efforts to bring people from the Muslim side and the Christian side together. This he believes to be the responsibility of religious institutions like Christian theological seminaries and the Muslim al-Azhar University. Up until today, very little has been done in this field. Whereas the Coptic Catholic Seminary has already invited Muslim professors from al-Azhar University several times, al-Azhar has not yet responded by inviting Christian professors to give lectures there in return.

8.1.2. Bishop Amba Maqar – The Coptic Orthodox Seminary, Cairo

His Excellency Amba Maqar is bishop of the Synod of Goshen of the Coptic Orthodox Church and head of the Coptic Orthodox Seminary (*Kuliyyat al-Lahut al-Orthuduksiyya al-Klirikiyya* in Arabic), located on the campus of the Cathedral of St. Mark in al-Abbasiyya, Cairo.[2] During the interview, other guests joined the conversation, including Professor Aida Nasif of Cairo University and Professor Adly Anis Solaiman of Cairo University.

With regard to Christian-Muslim relations, the bishop explains that the comparison of religions department of the Coptic Orthodox Seminary closed down in 2016. Orthodox officials no longer use the term "comparison of religions" (*muqāranat al-adyan* in Arabic) any more. Since 2016, Islam as a religion has not been taught as a subject at the seminary anymore either. The decision was taken in order to avoid any kind of misunderstanding or false interpretation. When asked how students could then acquire a knowledge of Islam, the bishop answers that the seminary provides a good library with a wide range of books concerning Islam, past and present. Students are supposed to study these resources on their own.

---

[2] Amba Maqar, interview by author, at the Coptic Orthodox Seminary in al-Abbasiyya, Cairo, March 24, 2019.

Nevertheless, the seminary does provide lectures in Islamic philosophy about classical Muslim philosophers like al-Kindi, Ibn Rushd, and others. In this regard, the seminary cooperates with professors of Cairo University like Aida Nasif, Professor of Philosophy, and Professor Adly Anis Solaiman, Professor of Geography. Weighing in on this point, Professor Nasif explained her understanding of the teaching of Islamic philosophy. To her, this approach is useful for broadening the horizons of students of both Muslim and Christian backgrounds. She understands philosophy as a field of thinking, as a cognitive exercise for proving different ideas but not requiring any strong obligations to agree to any one idea in particular. Therefore, this approach is different to a merely religious way of thinking. Professor Solaiman adds that his way of teaching geography also imparts knowledge about different cultures in history and in the present. His special interest is Christian people in the Middle East in both history and today. In his opinion, the more students get to know different cultures, the more they will be open to valuing them. Therefore, this is an indirect approach to a dialogical way of thinking. Like Professor Nasif, he stresses that it is useful not to focus on questions of creed, but to concentrate on other aspects of human cultures instead.

With regard to Christian doctrine, Amba Maqar states that the Coptic Orthodox Seminary focuses on the teachings of the church fathers in order to remain faithful to the roots of the church. The lectures are intended to enable students to explain and defend the Christian creed, Christian doctrine, and the Christian worldview. This is by no means meant as an attack on anybody else, but purely for the study of one's own faith in order to explain it in a proper way either to members of the Coptic Orthodox Church or to people who are atheists.

Asked about future challenges, the bishop answers that at least two problems must be addressed: firstly, the tendency of people not to take religion seriously, which in his words is the challenge of atheism. Secondly, moral issues are at stake. People have access to pornography via television and the internet. The church should devote its energy to face these challenges head-on. It is specially the youth that need to be supported to be able to live according to Christian ethics. Thirdly, the bishop also stresses the need to expand the social work of the church among poor people in society.

8.1.3. Dr. Atif Jindy – Director of the Evangelical Theological Seminary in Cairo

With regard to Christian-Muslim relations over the last decade, Dr. Jindy mentions that a number of violent incidents have taken place, such as the burning of churches or of Christian institutions, and especially in 2013.[3] But this should not be overemphasized, since a number of high officials in politics and society take a moderate stand towards Christians. In this sense, then, the situation remains somewhat ambiguous. Concerning the role of al-Azhar University, he explains that not only is the position of the Grand Imam of al-Azhar important, but also those of the

[3] Atif Jindy, interview by author, at the Evangelical Theological Seminary, Abbasiyya, Cairo, March 29, 2019.

Egyptian Minister of Religious Endowments and the Grand Mufti of Egypt. He states that it is difficult to ascribe any one particular role to al-Azhar, not only because of its size, but also because of the fact that its official statements may differ from what is actually taught there.

To his knowledge, reformist Islamic thinking has not been adopted by Azhari scholars to date. Whether they might do so in future is not clear at this point. Thus far there is no official cooperation between the seminary and al-Azhar, even though on the personal level there are some good relationships. The issue of dialogue does not seem to be an important topic to the scholars of al-Azhar thus far. Jindy states that the efforts of the Egyptian political leadership to improve interreligious discourse turn out to be very helpful, not only for the relations as such, but also with regard to symbolic issues, such as the building of New Cairo.[4] The fact that the government provided for the construction of a big mosque and a big cathedral clearly shows the intention of the political leadership to treat Muslims and Christians equally.

Furthermore, the Egyptian president occasionally visits Christian churches, usually at Christian feasts like Christmas. These activities of the political leadership contribute to the public discourse, since they result in Christians being represented in the public sphere. Jindy mentions another important point by saying that after the 2013 attacks, the Egyptian state took care of the reconstruction and renovation of destroyed Christian churches and institutions. This shows the public that in the eyes of the government, Christians are equal Egyptian citizens and part of the society, as they have been from the beginning. Director Jindy regards these governmental activities as being of utmost importance for interreligious relations and Christian-Muslim dialogue in particular, because they value Christians as an equal counterpart to Muslims.

8.1.4. Common Issues – A Comment

With regard to the interviews, at least two striking commonalities may be observed concerning the situation of Christians in Egypt. Firstly, the security situation of Christians: According to the interviewees, the security of Christians is always connected to the question of political power. If the political leadership protects Christians, then they are safe; when it becomes unstable, their situation normally worsens. The interviewees state that the current political situation has improved. Secondly, there is a felt need to prove that Christians are true Egyptians and part and parcel of the Egyptian heritage and society. This can be accomplished by taking responsibility for society. Therefore, for them, social work has not only a diaconical dimension, but also a political one in a certain sense.

None of the three seminaries currently have a department of comparative religion anymore. This is due to different reasons – either because of the desire to avoid misunderstandings, as in the case of the Coptic Orthodox Seminary, or to allow for a new approach to teaching, like in the case of the other two seminaries.

---

[4] See: https://en.m.wikipedia.org/wiki/New_Cairo (accessed July 20, 2019).

As far as the role of al-Azhar University is concerned, the interviewees did not mention any organized dialogical exchange efforts so far. Rather, some initiatives may be found on the level of cooperation with individuals, mostly as a kind of official dialogue in order to assure the willingness of both sides to foster and build on peaceful coexistence. A common hope is that in the near future, it will be possible to organize an exchange of professors from both sides – for al-Azhar scholars to teach courses on Islam at Christian seminaries, and for Christian scholars to deliver courses on Christianity at al-Azhar University.

8.2. Christian Church Officials

8.2.1. Refat Fathy – General Secretary of the Synod of the Nile (Presbyterian)

According to Rev. Refat Fathy, the situation of Christian churches in Egypt has changed for the better since the establishment of the Egyptian Council of Churches in 2013.[5] It is now easier for churches to cooperate, and the churches are able to speak with one voice about issues in the society. There are eighteen Protestant denominations in Egypt. The biggest are the Presbyterian Church (Nile Synod) with about 750,000 members and the Church of God, a Pentecostal church with approximately 200,000 members. The churches provide schools and hospitals that are widely accepted in Egyptian society.

Christian schools are especially known for academic excellence. At these schools, children from both Christian and Muslim backgrounds study together. The curricula are the same as those for public schools. Among other things, the schools aim to provide lectures on values like justice, peace, and tolerance in order to serve society.

Rev. Fathy says concerning interreligious matters that security depends to a great extent on the stability of the political situation. In the last years, progress has been made in this regard. With regard to al-Azhar University, Rev. Fathy is hopeful that good relations can be developed and expanded.

8.2.2. Dr. Tharwat Kades – Director of the International Academy of Dialogue

Concerning Christian-Muslim relations in Egypt, Dr. Tharwat Kades explains that the role of al-Azhar University has been an ambiguous one for a long time.[6] One reason for this might have been the influence of members of the Muslim Brotherhood. Things changed to a certain extent after the uprisings of 2011 and 2012. In 2012, the *Council of Ecumenical Relations and Dialogue* (*majlis al-hiwār wa*

---

[5] Refat Fathy, interview by author, at the headquarters of the Synod of the Nile, Cairo, March 26, 2019.

[6] Tharwat Kades, interview by author, at at the headquarters of the Synod of the Nile, Cairo, March 31, 2019.

al-'alāqāt al-maskūnīya in Arabic) was founded. Due to dialogical engagement as well as to personal contacts between Christian and Muslim scholars (both male and female), it was possible to start a cooperation between the Council and an Islamic institution in 2012. Under the auspices of Prof. Dr. Hoda Darwish, head of the *Comparative Religion Department* of Zagazig University, meetings between Christian and Muslim students were organized on a regular basis. Furthermore, Prof. Dr. Ikram Lamey was invited to deliver lectures on the history of Christianity at Zagazig University.

Over the years, the number of students attending these lectures steadily increased. At last count, there were about sixty students. Currently, cooperation between Zagazig University and al-Azhar University allows students of al-Azhar University to partake in courses delivered at the department chaired by Prof. Dr. Hoda Darwish and to acquire academic grades like Master's Degrees and Doctoral Degrees at the department.

In 2018, an *International Academy of Dialogue* was founded. Since the experiences were positive, it is the intention of both the *International Academy* and the *Comparative Religion Department* of Zagazig University to expand programs even more in the near future.

Concerning the academy, Dr. Kades states, firstly, that it is important for Muslims and Christians to approach each other on a scholarly level; secondly, that the academy is a voice within the field of political relations; and, thirdly, that the academy promotes social and official dialogue. In expanding a network of personal relations, the academy opens up new ways of cooperation in future.

8.2.3. Prof. Dr. Ikram Lamey – The Evangelical Theological Seminary, Cairo

Prof. Dr. Ikram Lamey points out that for several years, he had been active in writing a newspaper column on a weekly basis, commenting on different issues from a Christian perspective.[7] Furthermore, he states that he attempted to write in such a way that his texts could be understood by everyday readers. Because of his columns, he was asked by Zagazig University to deliver courses on Christian history. The idea was that the content of the Christian faith and praxis should be explained at the university's *Comparative Religion Department* by a Christian instead of by a Muslim scholar. According to Prof. Dr. Lamey, the historical approach allows him to explain the content of Christian belief and praxis within the framework of political, social, and other contexts.

After a time of observing and testing his way of teaching, this attempt proved to be fruitful also in the eyes of the university board. Therefore, since then, Dr. Lamey has taught a new course every semester. According to him, this is an exceptional case in that an Islamic university in Egypt allowed a Christian scholar to deliver courses on Christianity. To his knowledge, this project is unique in Egypt to date.

---

[7] Ikram Lamey, interview by author, at at the headquarters of the Synod of the Nile, Cairo, March 31, 2019.

9. Muslim Voices on Muslim-Christian Relations in Egypt 2019 – Interviews

9.1. Comparison of Religions at Universities

9.1.1. Prof. Dr. Hoda Darwish, Head of Comparative Religions, Zagazig University

Dr. Hoda Darwish mentions that she has been cooperating with the *Council of Ecumenical Relations and Dialogue* (*majlis al-hiwār wa al-'alāqāt al-maskūnīya* in Arabic) for a couple of years now. In this regard, the lectures on Christian history taught by Dr. Lamey at her department proved to be very fruitful. She says that it is not yet possible for a Christian professor to teach about Christian religion at al-Azhar University. Therefore, her department is breaking new ground. She is the head of the *Comparative Religion Department* (*qism al-adyan al-muqāran* in Arabic) and the *Center of Israeli Studies* (*markaz al-dirāsāt Israīlīyya* in Arabic).[1]

Dr. Darwish states that religions are quite often misused today to justify unjust deeds and violence. She also says that the comparison of religions should be aimed at showing that all religions share certain values, and that all of them deal with a wide range of issues that are important for people. Therefore, it is necessary for every religion to get as much knowledge about other religions as possible, in order to prevent prejudices and to promote cooperation.

Dr. Darwish emphasizes that according to the Qur'an, Islam recognizes all other heavenly religions, prophets, and messengers. Therefore, it should be normal for Islamic institutions to study the scriptures and other manifestations of various other religions, and for the institutions of other religions to do so as well. She declares that her institute provides teaching for qualified preachers and teachers of Islam (*du'āt* in Arabic) in order to correct the image of Islam all over the world and to teach Muslims about other religions. She adds that the teaching provided by her department should also address issues of atheism, extremism, and the negative influences of new media.

[1] Hoda Darwish, interview by author, at Zagazig University, Zagazig, Egypt, March 31, 2019.

9.1.2. Dr. Mohey El-Din Afifi, General-Secretary of the Council of Islamic Research,[2] Al-Azhar University

Dr. El-Din Afifi starts by outlining the history of dialogue in Islam and states that throughout Islamic history and beginning in the time of the prophet Muḥammad, dialogue played an important role. Even during times of struggle or war, dialogue efforts never ceased. The exchange of ideas has helped different civilizations to develop. He believes that dialogue is a task for all religions and all human beings.[3] He says that he has helped lead the *Faculty of Da'wah Islamiyya* of al-Azhar University in Cairo for years, and in particular the *Department of the Comparison of Religions* which forms part of this faculty. He emphasizes that al-Azhar University has taken part in dialogue activities with the Roman Catholic Church, as well as the Anglican Church and the World Council of Churches.

9.1.3. Dr. Jamal al-Farouq, Head of the Da'wah Faculty[4] of Al-Azhar University, Cairo

Dr. al-Farouq believes that the ground for dialogue according to the Qur'an is the call to *come to a common word* (Surah 5:64).[5] He states that in his faculty, the comparison of religions is taught using scholarly methods. On the question whether books about the method of comparison used in his faculty are available, he answers that this is not yet the case. He also states that it is not possible to invite a Christian scholar to al-Azhar to teach about Christianity. As a positive example of Christian-Muslim relations, he mentions *Family House* (*bayt al-'āila* in Arabic).

9.1.4. Dr. Adil Muḥammad Darwish, Director of Religions and Sects Department[6] of Al-Azhar University, Cairo

Dr. Darwish observes that in his department, first year students are taught about the heavenly religions, second year students about other religions, and third year students about different streams of Islam.[7] He says that verses from the Bible are also used to teach about Christianity. He states that it is important to maintain the balance between traditional thinking and new thinking. Asked for a book about the methodology used in the comparison of religions, he states that such a book is not yet available.

---

[2] *Mujamac al-buhūt̠ al-Islamīyya* in Arabic.

[3] Mohey El-Din Afifi, interview by author, Al-Azhar University, Cairo, April 1, 2019.

[4] *Kulliyat ad-da'wah islāmīyya* in Arabic.

[5] Jamal al-Farouq, interview by author, Al-Azhar University, Cairo, April 1, 2019.

[6] *Qism al-adyan wa al-mad̠āhib* in Arabic.

[7] Adil Muḥammad Darwish, interview by author, Al-Azhar University, Cairo, April 1, 2019.

9.2. Common Issues and Observations – A Comment

The Muslim interviewees are all high-ranking officials of either al-Azhar University or Zagazig University, which cooperates with al-Azhar University to a certain extent. With regard to the officials of al-Azhar, it may be noted that the interviews had to be conducted in Arabic. It seems that work in the field of the comparison of religions is undertaken at al-Azhar in the Arabic language only. Access to sources in English and in other languages seems to be very limited. It is not yet possible to study other religions based on research of their sources in their original languages (like ancient Hebrew, ancient Greek, Sanskrit, and others). Therefore, the comparison of religions at al-Azhar seems to focus either on acquiring a certain knowledge about these religions via secondary sources, or on different topics that are then compared.

The officials did not mention any well-known book or tract on the methodology of the comparison of religions, nor a particular scholar of al-Azhar who is a well-known representative of this field. This creates the impression that this is not an issue of any great importance to these institutions.

In comparison to al-Azhar, the attempts at Zagazig University seem to lead in a different direction. One comes away with the impression that Islamic research on other religions should be based on the language in which their sources are written. For instance, some of the doctoral students have learned Hebrew and English. The institute of Dr. Darwish envisages future cooperation with universities in other countries as soon as possible, in order to acquire language skills and to exchange knowledge, experience, and ideas.

Part III.

Towards a Better Understanding

Taken together, the interviews have shown that researchers and scholars on the Christian side attempt to promote interreligious dialogue in a variety of ways. Comparison of religions departments have been closed down in order to avoid misunderstandings. This reveals that it is difficult to promote interreligious exchanges in Egypt today. It has also become clear that the comparison of religions is not an important matter to officials of al-Azhar. In fact, resources on the comparison of religions are rare. Works like the books of Ḥimāiyah, Rayyān, and Shalabi are therefore no exceptions. They appear to represent a way of thinking that values the comparison of religions only for apologetic purposes. This raises the question as to how ways for a better future can be found. What kind of a methodology of comparison could be helpful?

10. Comparison of Religions in International Discourses

10.1. Comparison of Religions as a Means towards a Better Understanding

The analysis has shown that efforts of Muslim scholars like Ḥimāiyah, Rayyān, and Shalabi to understand Christian doctrine and the Christian worldview are confined to an entirely Islamic framework of thinking. This raises the question: What is required to understand a different religion according to its own standards? After all, it goes without saying that a better understanding is needed. The following sections will therefore deal with some important aspects of the comparison of religions as discussed in the international discourse. Due to spatial limitations, we have to confine ourselves to a selection of only a few methodological ideas.

10.2. Methodology of Comparison

10.2.1. On Interpreting the Religious Other: Four Conditions – Finn Collin

The academic Finn Collin suggests that if researchers try to understand a religious tradition and suppose that they have found some contradictions in it, then they should take into account the following four conditions of interpretation for the sake of a better understanding: the *veridicality condition*, the *reality condition*, the *parasitism condition*, and the *epistemic condition*.[1]

10.2.1.1. Veridicality Condition

According to Collin, it is helpful *hypothetically to assume* the other religion to be coherent. If a certain phenomenon appears illogical or even absurd to the interpreter, then he should search for an explanation from within the foreign religious tradition itself. The assumption is that the foreign religious tradition is logical and coherent in its own way, but that the researcher has not yet has been able to understand the inner logic of the religious tradition at stake. In assuming that there might be a coherency, the interpreter is urged to search for those aspects that he might

[1] Finn Collin, "Meta-Constraints upon Interpretation," *American Philosophical Quarterly* 24 (1987): 137-148.

have overlooked thus far. In other words: The veridicality condition is meant to be a hermeneutical principle in the sense that the interpreter is urged to reflect on his own way of thinking and on his own way of perceiving things, in order to distance himself from his ordinary way of thinking. In doing so, the interpreter might be able to find a coherence of thought and praxis different from his own.

10.2.1.2. Reality Condition

The second of Collins' conditions is called the *reality condition*. The interpreter might come across things she might deem to be absurd or meaningless. Again, the interpreter is urged hypothetically to presuppose that the very phenomenon that seems meaningless to her (a certain behavior or praxis of the religious Other, for instance) might have an importance in the lifeworld of the religious Other. The interpreter is urged to search for such meaning, that is, for the function of a certain phenomenon (a ritual, for instance) in the lifeworld of the religious Other. The presupposition is that there is a connection between this particular phenomenon and "reality." But what adherents of a different religious tradition perceive as *reality* might be different from the opinion or understanding of the interpreter. Again, the researcher is called to distance herself from her own way of thinking, her ordinary understanding of the world.

10.2.1.3. Parasitism Condition

The same holds true for the third condition, called the *parasitism condition*. The thesis is that the interpreter should not measure phenomena according to his own framework of thinking. In comparing phenomena of the foreign religion with his own culture and worldview, the researcher should abstain from comparing them with his own framework of thinking. Rather, he should seek to understand the *framework* of thinking of the foreign religious tradition according to *its own* standards. The phenomena have to be understood as far as possible *within* the framework of the different religion. The act of interpreting a religious phenomenon should therefore not be a kind of parasitism, that is, it should not be like a parasite living off of the resources of the host. The metaphor alludes to the operative framework of thinking. The act of interpretation should not rest on the assumptions of one's own worldview (which could be called parasitism), but on the assumptions of the foreign religion as far as one has proceeded to understand them.

10.2.1.4. Epistemic Condition

Finally, Finn speaks of the *epistemic condition*. The interpreter is called upon not to attribute information, knowledge, understanding, or capacities to members of a foreign religion which they could not have or could not have had. The interpreter is urged to reflect on things she might have ascribed to members of the foreign religion. Once again, the condition calls researchers to reflect carefully upon the assumptions they make.

By applying these four conditions to the question of the comparison of religions undertaken by Muslim scholars, one may hope that a number of misunderstandings can be avoided in the future.

10.2.2. The Need to Distance Oneself from One's Own Worldview

A proper comparison of religions depends on the willingness and ability of the researcher to abstain from judging everything only according to his own religious truth claims. As has been shown, none of the abovementioned al-Azhar scholars seems willing or able to work according to this methodological principle. Therefore, all of these approaches are to be labeled as apologetic. Why then was it necessary or even desirable to deal with approaches such as those of Ḥimāiyah, Rayyān, or Shalabi?

The answer is that people in Western societies, and particularly people who are engaged in interreligious relations and interreligious dialogue, ought to know how well-known scholars of the other religious camp think. Even though a number of Muslim thinkers, both male and female, may indeed be labeled as "reformist," these thinkers are in no way the majority among Muslim scholars. Therefore Western audiences and Christian observers not acquainted with the situation in countries like Egypt need to be aware of the wide range of opinions represented there. The apologetic approaches of Ḥimāiyah, Rayyān, and Shalabi collectively may legitimately be called "mainstream thinking" for the ranks of scholars at al-Azhar University. People in the West should be aware of just how difficult it is to talk about interreligious dialogue in a majority Muslim country like Egypt. To believe that "dialogue" in Egypt means the same as it does in Western countries is an illusion. The interviews have shown how difficult the current situation is.

Scholarly work has to take into account not only the rare examples of so-called "liberal" thinkers in Islam, but also the majority opinion of Christians as represented by ordinary scholars like Ḥimāiyah, Rayyān, and Shalabi. Their attitude is apologetic. Their lack of information on Christian scriptures, doctrinal traditions, and theological thinking has become strikingly clear. The same goes for their lack of language skills and of willingness to apply new hermeneutical methods, if such methods are known to them in the first place.

Taking this into account, the question is how Muslims and Christians may proceed to build good relations with each other. One may argue that it would be sufficient simply to assure the Other of friendly relations, as is done in official dialogues, or to focus only on social matters, as is done in social dialogues. But confining oneself to these kinds of dialogues would mean leaving out the most important point, namely, the theological basis for the rather negative attitude towards the religious Other, an attitude that arises from adhering to outdated apologetic traditions and instincts.

What is needed, then, is not for either side to relativize its point of view or religious convictions. What is needed is for each side to let its own religious worldview be accompanied by a different perspective. This perspective may be ethical, philosophical, or historical. One may maintain one's own convictions, but engaging in a proper comparison of religions would mean to allow it to be accompanied by a different perspective, that is, a non-religious view of the matter at stake. Whether Muslim scholars will be open to such an endeavor remains to be seen. The example of Dr. Darwish, head of the comparative religions department at Zagazig University shows that there is reason to hope.

10.2.3. The Need to Differentiate between Different Levels of Agreement and Disagreement

A proper comparison of religions requires that the religious worldview of the researcher must be left aside as much as possible while she scrutinizes the phenomena at stake. One may add that it is also necessary for her to differentiate between different levels of agreement and disagreement between different religions. There may be phenomena where commonalities and agreement may be attested to some degree, while there may also be major differences about certain other phenomena.

When it comes to matters of doctrine, it may well be that the factor of disagreement predominates. Nevertheless, some phenomena may still be compared without invoking a sense of competition. This may hold true for questions of philosophy, for instance, since philosophy is often regarded as a kind of playground for experiments of human reasoning. It may be that in this field, people do not argue as strongly along lines of true and false, but rather along lines of an argument being convincing or not convincing, or along the line of it being logically coherent or less coherent. In the following section, we will engage in considerations about the levels of ethical, philosophical, and historical research and discussion.

10.3. Christian-Muslim Dialogue on the Comparison of Religions – Prospects

10.3.1. Non-apologetic Comparison

To undertake the comparison of religions as a non-apologetical enterprise will surely open up new opportunities for listening to each other and learning from each other. Doing so should not be interpreted as an attempt to relativize religious truth claims, but rather as an attempt to locate them in a wider framework. One may, for example, as a Muslim scholar adhere to the belief that the Christian notion of Christ as the son of God is unacceptable for Muslims. Nevertheless, a non-apologetic approach could value – in an ethical perspective – the fact that ethically, Christians do not strive for revenge, since they trace the need for forgiveness and reconciliation back to their understanding of the Christ event as the reconciliation between God and humankind. That would mean that even though the Muslim scholar would continue to reject the Christian doctrine, he may simultaneously value its ethical consequences. The same holds true for other levels of comparison.

10.3.2. Comparison of Religions from an Ethical Perspective

The prospect of comparing ethical principles would be oriented towards an attempt to find common ground with regard to core values like justice and peace. The task ahead then is to define more closely what a concept like justice in particular means. There is an open space for scholars on both sides to explain to each other the theological basis for different ethical concepts. For instance, there may be open ground in not arguing that sharia law entails certain eternal rules that must necessarily be followed in the same manner until the end of time. Instead, it may be helpful to concentrate on the principles of the *higher objectives* of sharia law (*maqāṣid as-sharia* in Arabic) as proposed by a number of Muslim scholars. *Mohammad Omar Farooq*, for instance, writes:

> If the Muslim Ummah is to meet challenges contemporary to each generation the Muslims need to reconnect themselves to Islam by repositioning the Qur'an at the ***center*** of their understanding and commitment. The Qur'an provides relatively few legal precepts. However, manifest within its message is a value-oriented approach from which a set of values can be extracted that is universal in nature. ... Such value-orientation would enable better praxis in terms of the higher objective – *maqāṣid* – of Islam. In this context, the term *Maqāṣid al-Islām*, instead of *Maqāṣid al-Sharī'ah*, should be used. The dynamism engendered in this radical alternative would free Muslims from the insularity of their current text-orientation, which is a significant factor responsible for their stagnation.[2]

This is only one example of a field of discussion that could break new ground in Christian-Muslim relations.

10.3.3. Comparison of Religions in Philosophical Perspectives

A second non-apologetic approach to the comparison of religions could be undertaken in the field of philosophical thinking. As mentioned above, it is necessary to understand the framework of thinking of a particular religious tradition. As we have seen, none of the authors discussed shows any willingness to try to understand Christian teachings according to their own understanding. The predominant view is that Christian theology and doctrine are illogical, childish, and foolish. Human reason rejects these teachings, the authors argue. Often in apologetic literature, a conspiracy theory is at stake, such as the notion that Christian monks or priests tried to maintain these illogical teachings out of greed and for reason of personal advantages. These apologetic arguments have a long history in Islamic thinking.

The challenge then is to compare different aspects of Muslim and Christian thinking concerning philosophical challenges that arise whenever human reasoning is concerned with certain principles. Take for instance the question of how the eternal and transcendent God can reveal himself without being involved in affairs of creation. How can something be deemed to be with God or alongside God, that is, be with God before the creation of the universe, like the *Logos* in Christian

[2] Mohammad Omar Farooq, "Conclusion: Toward Our Reformation," in id., *Toward our Reformation: From Legalism to Value-Oriented Islamic Law and Jurisprudence* (London: The International Institute of Islamic Thought, 2011), 270-271.

theology and the *umm al-kitāb* in Muslim understanding? Are there not on both sides philosophical challenges, questions, logical inconsistencies, and suchlike? In a philosophical discussion, it would not be a matter of who is right and who is wrong. The question would be: How can the human mind, the mind of a creature, grasp the eternal truth of God? Once again, this is meant only as an example for a non-apologetic approach to the comparison of religions.

10.3.4. Comparison of Religions in Historical Perspectives

A third kind of comparison would be a historical one. The problem at stake is summarized by the scholar Nicolai Sinai:

> The Qur'an, so Islamic sources and traditional Western scholarship tell us, did not come into existence all at once but was revealed over a period of some twenty-two years. From a religious perspective, of course, this historical spread might seem accidental, especially when viewed as the manifestation of a pre-given *umm al-kitāb* that stands above the vicissitudes of history. However, any attempt at reading the Qur'an without falling back on religious premises of this kind will of necessity have to take the processual genesis of the text much more seriously, i.e., as potentially affecting both its linguistic configuration and its theological and anthropological content – if, that is, the attempt of a chronological ordering of the Qur'anic corpus does not itself rest on faith rather than argument.[3]

Comparison of religions in a historical perspective would mean to make use of the methodological tools of historical scholarship. If one is open at least to testing some of these methods, questions like the following would arise: With what kind of Christians may Muḥammad have been in contact? Could it be that Muḥammad adopted Christian traditions and incorporated them into the Qur'anic message? Was Muḥammad simply the transmitter of a fixed text, or was he the transmitter of a divine impulse which he expressed in his own words? Is Muḥammad alone the "author" of the Qur'anic text? Could it be that instead, Muḥammad "responded" to the questions and the needs of the early *Muslim community* he led ? Could this *interaction* between Muḥammad, his opponents, and his community of believers have been the very medium Allah chose to reveal his message?

Could the depictions of 'Īsā and Mary in the Qur'an perhaps serve different purposes in arguing with Jewish and Christian groups in Medina? Could there have been a development of the images of 'Īsā and Mary in the Qur'an?[4] And

---

[3] Nicolai Sinai, "The Qur'an as Process," in Angelika Neuwirth, Nicolai Sinai, and Michael Marx, eds., *The Qur'ān in Context: Historical and Literary Investigations into the Qur'ānic Milieu* (Leiden: Brill, 2011), 407.

[4] Angelika Neuwirth, "The House of Abraham and the House of Amram: Genealogy, Patriarchal Authority, and Exegetical Professionalism," in Neuwirth, Sinai, and Marx, eds., *The Qur'ān in Context*, 499-531; id., "Mary and Jesus – Counterbalancing the Biblical Patriarchs: A Re-reading of Sūrat Āl-'Imrān (3:1-62)," *Parole de l' Orient* 30 (2005): 231-260.

if so, what would that mean? Could the Qur'anic arguments perhaps not really have orthodox Christian theology in mind? Could they have been directed against certain "Christian" groups which the ancient Christian church would have called heretical? Questions like these would open up a new field of discussion. If these discussions were to be understood not as undermining the Muslim faith, but simply as a wider range of information about the historical circumstances, then the comparison of religions could serve as a countermeasure against merely apologetic arguments. In countries like Turkey, it is possible to discuss such questions to a certain degree. Whether this will be possible in Egypt in the near future remains uncertain.

10.3.5. Comparison of Religions and the Future of Dialogue – A Conclusion

The first part of this work aimed to show how important al-Azhar University is within the Egyptian context and beyond. The second part was devoted to studying the comparison of religions as undertaken by three scholars who trained at al-Azhar and who served on the staff of al-Azhar University for at least a period of time. The outcome of this study was that all three authors, Ḥimāiyah, Rayyān, and Shalabi understand their work as a kind of comparison of religions. As has been shown, their approaches vary, since the first author can be labeled as employing direct comparison, the second indirect comparison, and the third historical comparison. All three are apologetic in tone and do not perceive Christian scriptures, doctrines and theological thinking on the basis of Christian theology, but solely on the basis of an Islamic framework of thinking. The interviews showed that it is currently very difficult to undertake any kind of comparison of religions in Egypt that is non-apologetic.

Nevertheless, we must be aware that these authors represent Egyptian Islamic mainstream thinking about People of the Book, and especially about Christians. Therefore, it is important for Western readers to understand that Muslim reformist thinkers in Western countries are by no means representative of the majority of Islamic thinking today. We must know this in order to understand the current situation in Egypt, to understand the challenges lying ahead, and to understand the attitude of a number of Muslims with regard to Christians or Jews. In short: It is necessary to understand how serious the challenges are in order to respond in a proper way. What is needed are new ways of comparison that would open up new ways for dialogical relations. A non-apologetic approach is vitally needed.

It is my hope that in future, reforms at al-Azhar University will lead not only to the establishment of departments for ancient languages like Greek and Hebrew in order for students to learn about Christian and Jewish sources, but also to the establishment of departments for religious studies that are not concerned mainly with Muslim apologetics, but with broadening horizons in order to explore new fields of dialogical thinking.

11. Bibliography

Abd al-Wahhab, Ahmad. *Al-masih fi masadir al-aqaid al-masihiyya*. Cairo, 1988.

———. *Christ as Seen in the Sources of the Christian Beliefs*. 2nd ed. Cairo: Wahba Book Shop, 1985.

Abū-Nimer, Mohammed. *Unity in Diversity: Interfaith Dialogue in the Middle East*. Washington, DC: United States Institute of Peace Press, 2007, 141-178.

Abū Rayya, Muḥammad. *Din allah wahid – muhammad wa'l-masih akhawan*. Cairo: Dar al-karnak, 1963.

———. *Din allah wahid – 'ala alsina jami' al rusul*. 2nd ed. Cairo: Alam al-kutub, 1970.

Abū Zahra, Muḥammad. *Muhadarat fi'-nasraniyya*. 5th ed. Cairo: Dar alfikr al-'arabi, 1977.

Accad, M. "Corruption and/or Misinterpretation of the Bible: The Story of the Islamic Usage of Tahrif." *Theological Review* 24 (2003):67-97.

———. "Muḥammad's Advent as the Final Criterion for the Authenticity of the Judaeo-Christian Tradition: Ibn Qayyim al-Jawziyya's Hidayat al-Hayara fi Ajwibat al-Yahud wa-l-Nasara." In *The Three Rings: Textual Studies in the Historical Trialogue of Judaism, Christianity, and Islam*. Edited by Barbara Roggema, Marcel Poorthuis, and Pim Valkenberg. Leuven: Uitgeverij Peeters, 2005, 217-236.

Adang, Camilla. "Medieval Muslim Polemics against the Jewish Scripture." In *Muslim Perceptions of Other Religions: A Historical Survey*. Edited by Jean Jacques Waardenburg. Oxford: Oxford University Press, 1999, 143-159.

Al-Khatib, Abd al-Karim. "Christ in the Qur'an, the Taurat, and the Injil." *The Muslim World* 61 (1971): 90-101.

Al-Saqqa, Ahmad Hijazi. *Aqanim al-Nasara*. Cairo: Dar al-Ansar, 1977.

Bano, Masooda. "Protector of the 'al-Wasatiyya' Islam: Cairo's al-Azhar University." In *Shaping Global Islamic Discourses: The Role of al-Azhar, al-Medina and al-Mustafa*. Edited by Masooda Bano and Keiko Sakurai. Edinburgh: Edinburgh University Press, 2015, 73-90.

Barraclough, Steven. "Al-Azhar: Between the Government and the Islamists." *Middle East Journal* 52 (1998): 236-249.

Becker, Carl Heinrich. "Christliche Polemik und islamische Dogmenbildung." *Zeitschrift für Assyriologie und vorderasiatische Archäologie* 26 (1912): 175-195.

Boase, Roger. "Autobiography of a Muslim Convert: Anselm Turmeda (c.1353-c.1430)." In *Al-Masāq: Studia Arabo-Islamica Mediterranea*. Vol. 9. Leeds: Department of Modern Arabic Studies, University of Leeds, 1996/7, 45-98.

Brown, Nathan J. *Post-Revolutionary al-Azhar*. Washington, DC: Carnegie Endowment for International Peace, 2011.

———. “Islam in Egypt’s Cacophonous Constitutional Order.” In *The Rule of Law, Islam, and Constitutional Politics in Egypt and Iran*. Edited by Said Amir Arjomand and Nathan J. Brown. New York: State University of New York Press, 2013, 233-248.

———. *Official Islam in the Arab World: The Contest for Religious Authority*. Washington, DC: Carnegie Endowment for International Peace, 2017.

Brunner, Rainer. “The Dispute About the Falsification of the Qur’an Between Sunnis and Shi’is in the 20th Century.” In *Studies in Arabic and Islam*. Edited by Stefan Leder, Hilary Kilpatrick, Bernadette Martel-Thoumian, and Hannelore Schönig. Orientalia Lovaniensia Analecta. Leuven: Uitgeverij Peeters 2002, 437-446.

Buhl, Frants. *The Encyclopaedia of Islam*. Vol. 4, s.v. “Taḥrīf.” Leiden: Brill, 1934.

Burton, John. “The Exegesis of Q. 2:106 and the Islamic Theories of Naskh: Mā nansakh min āya aw nansaha na’ti bi khairin minhā aw mithlihā.” *Bulletin of the School of Oriental and African Studies* 48 (1985): 452-469.

———. “The Interpretation of Q. 87, 6-7 and the Theories of Naskh.” *Der Islam* 62 (1985): 5-19.

———. “The Corruption of the Scriptures.” *Occasional Papers of the School of Abbasid Studies* 4 (1992, publ. 1994): 95-106.

Bütler, Robert A. “The Image of Christ in Recent Muslim Literature,” In id., *Trying to Respond: Essays and Reviews on Islam, Pakistan, and Christianity*. Edited by Muḥammad Ikrām Chaghatai. Lahore: Pakistan Jesuit Society, 1994, 389-408.

Calder, Norman. “Tafsir from Tabari to Ibn Kathir: Problems in the Description of a Genre, Illustrated with Reference to the Story of Abraham.” In *Approaches to the Qur’an*. Edited by Gerald R. Hawting and Abdul-Kader A. Shareef. London: Routledge, 1993, 101–40.

Campanini, Massimo. “Qur’anic Hermeneutics and Political Hegemony: Reformation of Islamic Thought.” *Muslim World* 2009: 124–33.

Charfi, Abdelmajid. “Christianity in the Qur’an Commentary of Tabari.” *Islamochristiana* 6 (1980): 105-148.

Collin, Finn. “Meta-Constraints upon Interpretation.” *American Philosophical Quarterly* 24 (1987): 137-148.

Deedat, Ahmed. *The Choice: Islam and Christianity*. Vol. 1. Doha: Fahil Khair, 1994.

El Khawaga, Dina. “The Political Dynamics of the Copts: Giving the Community an Active Role.” In *Christian Communities in the Arab Middle East: The Challenge of the Future*. Edited by Andrea Pacini. Oxford: Clarendon Press, 2004, 172-190.

Elsässer, Sebastian. “Press Liberalization, the New Media, and the “Coptic Question”: Muslim-Coptic Relations in Egypt in a Changing Media Landscape.” *Middle Eastern Studies* 46 (2010): 131-150.

Esack, Farid. “Qur’anic Hermeneutics: Problems and Prospects.” *Muslim World* 83, no.2 (1993): 118–41.

Farooq, Mohammad Omar. “Conclusion: Toward Our Reformation.” In id., *Toward our Reformation: From Legalism to Value-Oriented Islamic Law and Ju-*

risprudence, London: The International Institute of Islamic Thought, 2011, 260-272.
Ford, F. Peter Jr. "Abbas Mahmud al-Aqqad: The Genius of Christ." In *Studies in Contemporary Philosophical Theology.* Translated and edited by F. Peter Ford, Jr. Binghampton, NY: Global Publications, 2001.
Galal, Lise Paulsen. "Coptic Christian Practices: Formations of Sameness and Difference." *Islam and Christian-Muslim Relations* 23 (2012): 45-58.
Goddard, Hugh. "Contemporary Egyptian Muslim Views of Christianity." *Renaissance and Modern Studies* 31 (1987): 74-86.
———. "An annotated bibliography of works about Christianity by Egyptian Muslim Authors." *The Muslim World* 80 (1990): 251-277.
———. "The Persistence of Medieval Themes in Modern Christian-Muslim Discussion in Egypt." In *Christian Arabic Apologetics during the Abbasid Period (750-1258).* Edited by S. Khalil Samir and Jørgen S. Nielsen. Leiden: Brill, 1994, 225-237.
———. *Muslim Perceptions of Christianity.* London: Grey Seal, 1996.
Goldziher, Ignaz. "Über muhammedansche Polemik gegen Ahl al-kitab." *Zeitschrift der Deutschen Morgenländischen Gesellschaft* 32 (1878): 341-387.
Guillaume, A. "The Version of the Gospels in Medina circa 700 A.D." *Al-Andalus* 15 (1950): 289-296.
Haddad, Yvonne. "Muhammad Abduh: Pioneer of Islamic Reform." In *Pioneers of Islamic Revival.* Edited by Ali Rahnema. London: Atlantic Highlands, 1994, 30-63.
Halm, Heinz. *Die Kalifen von Kairo: Die Fatimiden in Ägypten 973-1074.* Munich: Beck, 2003.
Hamdan, Hussein. *Der christlich-islamische Dialog der Azhar-Universität.* Freiburg: Herder, 2014.
Hansen, Hendrik Lindberg. *Christian-Muslim Relations in Egypt: Politics, Society and Interfaith Encounters.* London: I.B. Tauris, 2015.
Hasan, Sonia S. *Christians versus Muslims in Modern Egypt: The Century-Long Struggle for Coptic Equality.* Oxford: Oxford University Press, 2003.
Hatina, Meir. "Historical Legacy and the Challenge of Modernity in the Middle East: The Case of al-Azhar in Egypt." *The Muslim World* 93 (2003): 51-68.
Ḥimāiyah, Maḥmūd ʻAlī ʻAbdel Raḥmān. *Tatlīṯ bayna al-waṯanīya wa al-masīḥīya.* Cairo: Dar al-Maʻarif, 2005.
Hirschkind, Charles. "Cassette Ethics: Public Piety and Popular Media in Egypt." In *Religion, Media, and the Public Sphere.* Edited by Birgit Meyer and Annelies Moors. Bloomington, IN: Indiana University Press, 2006, 29-51.
Iskander, Milad. "The Coptic Struggle after the Revolution of 1952." In *Copts in Egypt: A Christian Minority under Siege.* Edited by Martyn Thomas, Adly A. Youssef, Heinz Gstrein, and Paul Meinrad Strässle. Zurich: G2W-Verlag, 2006, 36-44.
Kairanvi, Maulana Rahmatullah. *Izhar' ul-Haqq: The Truth Revealed.* Parts 1-4. London: Ta Ha Publishers, 1989/90.

Krämer, Gudrun. “Die Islamische Welt im 20. Jahrhundert.” In *Der islamische Orient: Grundzüge seiner Geschichte*. Edited by Albrecht Noth and Jürgen Paul. Würzburg: Ergon, 1998, 439-504.

Künstlinger, Dawid. “Die Namen der ‘Gottes-Schriften’ im Qurān.” *Rocznik Orientalistyczny* 8 (1937): 72-84.

Kuhn, Michael F. “Early Islamic Perspectives of the Apostle Paul as a Narrative Framework for Taḥrīf.” In *Arab Christians and the Qur'an from the Origins of Islam to the Medieval Period*. Edited by Mark Beaumont. Leiden: Brill, 2018, 150-173.

Lazarus-Yafeh, Hava. “Is There a Concept of Redemption in Islam?” In *Types of Redemption*. Edited by R.J. Zwi Werblowsky and Claas Jouco Bleeker. Leiden: Brill, 1970, 168-180.

———. *Intertwined Worlds: Medieval Islam and Bible Criticism*. Princeton: Princeton University Press, 1992.

———. “Some Neglected Aspects of Medieval Muslim Polemics against Christianity.” *Harvard Theological Review* 89 (1996): 61-84.

———. *The Encyclopedia of Islam*. Vol. 10, s.v. “Taḥrif.” Leiden: Brill, 2000.

Leirvik, Oddbjørn. “Jesus in Modern Muslim Thought: From Anticolonial Polemics to Postcolonial Dialogue?” In *Jesus beyond Nationalism. Constructing the Historical Jesus in a Period of Cultural Complexity*. Edited by Halvor Moxnes, Ward Blanton, and James G. Crossley. London: Equinox Publishing, 2010.

Makari, Peter E. *Conflict and Cooperation: Christian-Muslim Relations in Contemporary Egypt*. Syracuse Studies on Peace and Conflict Resolution. Syracuse: Syracuse University Press, 2007.

McAuliffe, Jane Dammen. “Ibn Taymiya Treatiṣe on the Principles of Tafsir.” In *Windows on the House of Islam: Muslim Sources on Spirituality and Religious Life*. Edited by John Renard. Berkeley: University of California Press, 1998, 35–43.

———. “Ibn al-Jawzi's Exegetical Propaedeutic: Introduction and Translation of the (muqaddimah to Zad al-masir fi'ilm al-Tafsir). *Alif, Journal of Comparative Poetics* 8 (1988): 101–13.

———. “Qur'anic Hermeneutics: The Views of al-Tabari and Ibn Kathir.” In *Approaches to the History of the Interpretation of the Qur'an*. Edited by Andrew Rippin. Oxford: Clarendon Press, 1988, 46-62.

———. “The Qur'anic Context of Muslim Biblical Scholarship.” *Islam and Christian-Muslim Relations* 7 (1996): 141-158.

McCallum, Fiona. “Muslim-Christian Relations in Egypt: Challenges for the Twenty-First Century.” In *Christian Responses to Islam: Muslim-Christian Relations in the Modern World*. Edited by Anthony O'Mahony and Emma Loosley. Manchester: Manchester University Press, 2008.

Moltmann, Jürgen. *The Trinity and the Kingdom: The Doctrine of God*. Translated by Margaret Kohl. San Francisco: Harper, 1991.

Musa, Aisha Y. “The Qur'anists.” *Religion Compass* 4 (2010): 12-21.

Neuwirth, Angelika. "Mary and Jesus – Counterbalancing the Biblical Patriarchs: A Re-reading of Sūrat Āl-'Imrān (3:1-62)." *Parole de l' Orient* 30 (2005): 231-260.
———. "The House of Abraham and the House of Amram: Genealogy, Patriarchal Authority, and Exegetical Professionalism," In *The Qur'ān in Context: Historical and Literary Investigations into the Qur'ānic Milieu.* Edited by Angelika Neuwirth, Nicolai Sinai, and Michael Marx. Leiden: Brill, 2011, 499-531.
Nickel, Gordon D. "'We will Make Peace with You': The Christians of Najran in Muqatil's Tafsir." *Collectanea Christiana Orientalia* 3 (2006): 1-18.
———. "Early Muslim Accusations of Taḥrīf: Muqātil ibn Sulaymān's Commentary on Key Qur'anic Verses." In *The Bible in Arab Christianity.* Edited by David Thomas. Leiden: Brill, 2007, 207-223.
———. "'A Common Word' in Context: Toward the Roots of Polemics between Christians and Muslims in Early Islam." *Collectanea Christiana Orientalia* 6 (2009): 167-200.
———. "The Language of Love in Qur'an and Gospel." In *Sacred Text: Explorations in Lexicography.* Edited by Juan Pedro Monferrer-Sala and Ángel Urbán. Frankfurt: Peter Lang, 2009, 223-248.
———. *Narratives of Tampering in the Earliest Commentaries of the Qur'an.* Leiden: Brill, 2011.
Nolin, K. "Review of Abd al-Karim al-Khatib: Al-masih fi-l-Qur'an wa-l-tawrah wa-l-injil." *The Muslim World* 59 (1969): 74-79.
Ohlander, Erik. "Modern Qur'anic Hermeneutics." *Religion Compass* 3 (2009): 620-636.
Parolin, Gianluca P. "Al-Azhar (?) on Fundamental Freedoms." *Islamochristiana* 38 (2012): 117-127.
Pink, Johanna. "Tradition, Authority and Innovation in Contemporary Sunnī *tafsīr*: Towards a Typology of Qur'an Commentaries from the Arab World, Indonesia and Turkey." *Journal of Qur'anic Studies* 12 (2010): 56-82.
Powers, David. "The Exegetical Genre nasikh al-Qur'an Wa-manukhuhu." In *Approaches to the History of the Interpretation of the Qur'an.* Edited by Andrew Rippin. Oxford: Clarendon Press, 1988, 117–38.
Pulcini, Theodore. *Exegesis as Polemical Discourse: Ibn Ḥazm on Jewish and Christian Scriptures.* Atlanta: Scholars Press, 1998.
Rahman, Yusuf. "Hermeneutics of al-Baydawi in his Anwar al-tanzil wa asrar al-ta'wil." *Islamic Culture* 71, no.1 (1997): 1–14.
Rayyān, 'Alī Ṭāhā. *Al Masīḥ ibn Maryam fī al-qur'ān al karīm.* Cairo 2013.
Rock-Singer, Aaron. "Amr Khaled: From Da'wa to Political and Religious Leadership." *The British Journal of Middle Eastern Studies* 37 (2010): 15-37.
———. "A Pious Public: Islamic Magazines and Revival in Egypt, 1976-1981." *The British Journal of Middle Eastern Studies* 42 (2015): 427-46.
———. "The Salafi Mystique: The Rise of Gender Segregation in 1970s Egypt." *Islamic Law and Society* 23 (2016): 279-305.
———. "Censoring the Kishkophone: Religion and State Power in Mubarak's Egypt." *The International Journal of Middle East Studies* 49 (2017): 437-456.

Roniger, Luis. “Political Clientelism, Democracy, and Market Economy.” *Comparative Politics* 36 (2004): 353-375.

Roth, Norman. “Forgery and Abrogation of the Torah: A Theme in Muslim and Christian Polemic in Spain.” *Proceedings of the American Academy for Jewish Research* 54 (1987): 203-236.

Rowe, Paul. “Building Coptic Civil Society: Christian Groups and the State in Mubarak’s Egypt.” *Middle Eastern Studies* 45 (2009): 111-126.

Saeed, Abdullah. “Some Reflections on the Contextualist Approach to Ethico-Legal Texts of the Quran.” *Bulletin of the School of Oriental and African Studies* 71, no.2, (2008): 221–37.

———. “The Charge of Distortion of Jewish and Christian Scriptures.” *The Muslim World* 92 (2002): 419-436.

Scheepers, Phillip. “An Analysis of the Christology of Sheikh Ahmed Deedat.” *Vox Reformata* 2016: 1-30.

Schirrmacher, Christine. “The Influence of German Biblical Criticism on Muslim Apologetics in the Nineteenth Century.” In *A Comprehensive Faith: An International Festschrift for Rousas John Rushdoony*. Edited by Andrew Sandlin. San Jose, CA: Friends of Chalcedon, 1996, 107-121.

———. “The Influence of Higher Bible Criticism on Muslim Apologetics in the Nineteenth Century.” In *Muslim Perceptions of Other Religions: A Historical Survey*. Edited by Jean Jacques Waardenburg. Oxford: Oxford University Press, 1999, 270-279.

Schölch, Alexander. “Der arabische Osten im neunzehnten Jahrhundert 1800-1914.” In *Geschichte der arabischen Welt.* 5th edition. Edited by Ulrich Haarmann and Heinz Halm. Munich: Beck, 2004, 365-431.

Sedra, Paul. “Class Cleavages and Ethnic Conflict: Coptic Christian Communities in Modern Egyptian Politics.” *Islam and Christian-Muslim Relations* 10 (1999): 219-233.

Sellheim, Rudolf. “Prophet, Caliph und Geschichte: Die Muḥammad-Biographie des Ibn Ishaq.” *Oriens* 18-19 (1967): 33-91.

Shahin, E. E. *The Oxford Encyclopedia of the Modern Islamic World.* Vol. 3, s.v. “Rashid Riḍā, Muḥammad.” Oxford: Oxford University Press, 1995.

Shalabi, Ahmad. *Al-Masīḥīya – Muqāranat al-Adyan*. Vol. 2. 8th ed. Cairo: Dār al-Ma‘ārif, 2018.

Sinai, Nicolai. “The Qur’an as Process.” In *The Qur’ān in Context: Historical and Literary Investigations into the Qur’ānic Milieu.* Edited by Angelika Neuwirth, Nicolai Sinai, and Michael Marx. Leiden: Brill, 2011, 407-439.

Sirry, Mun’im, Scriptural Polemics. The Qur’ān and Other Religions, Oxford: Oxford University Press, 2014, 100-132.

Skovgaard-Petersen, Jakob. “Islamic Fundamentalism in Arab Television: Islamism and Salafism in Competition.” In *Fundamentalism in the Modern World: Fundamentalism and Communication; Culture, Media and the Public Sphere*. Edited by Ulrika Mårtensson. London: Tauris, 2011, 264-291.

———. “Egypt’s ‘Ulama in the State, in Politics, and in the Islamist Vision.” In *The Rule of Law, Islam, and Constitutional Politics in Egypt and Iran*. Edited by

Said Amir Arjomand and Nathan J. Brown. New York: State University of New York Press, 2013, 279-302.
Smith, David E. "The Structure of al-Baqarah." *The Muslim World* 91 (2001): 121-136.
Smith, Susan J. "Soundscapes." *Blackwell Publishing for the Royal Geographical Society with IBG* 26 (1994): 232-240.
Steinschneider, Moritz. *Polemische und apologetische Literatur in arabischer Sprache zwischen Muslimen, Christen und Juden, nebst Anhängen verwandten Inhalts*. Hildesheim: Olms, 1966.
Thomas, David. "The Bible in Early Muslim Anti-Christian Polemic." *Islam and Christian-Muslim Relations* 7 (1996): 29-38.
Troll, Christian. "A New Light on Christian-Muslim Controversy of the Nineteenth and Twentieth Century." *Die Welt des Islams* 34 (1994): 85-88.
Tworuschka, Udo. "Das Vergleichen von Religionen." In *Ökumene und Religionswissenschaft*. Edited by Ulrich Becker and Udo Tworuschka. Stuttgart: Calwer, 2006, 139-147.
Van Nispen tot Sevenaer, Christiaan. "Changes in Relations between Copts and Muslims (1952-1994) in the Light of the Historical Experience." In *Between Desert and City: The Coptic Orthodox Church Today*. Edited by Nelly van Doorn-Harder and Kari Vogt. Oslo: Novus Forlag, 2004.
Westlund, David. "Ahmed Deedat's Theology of Religion: Apologetics through Polemics." *Journal of Religion in Africa* 33 (2003): 263-278.
Wild, Stefan. "An Arabic Recitation: The Meta-Linguistics of Qur'anic Revelation." In *Self-Referentiality in the Qur'an*. Edited by Stefan Wild. Wiesbaden: Harrassowitz, 2006, 135-157.
Wilde, C. "Is there Room for Corruption of the 'Books' of God?" In *The Bible in Arab Christianity*. Edited by David Thomas. Leiden: Brill, 2007, 225-240.
Wrogemann, Henning. *A Theology of Interreligious Relations*. Translated by Karl E. Böhmer. Downers Grove, IL: IVP Academic, 2019.
Zahniser, A.-H. Mathias. "Major Transitions and Thematic Borders in Two long Suras: al-Baqara and al-Nisa." In *Literary Structures of Religious Meaning in the Qur'an*. Edited by Issa J. Boullata. Richmond: Curzon, 2000, 26-55.
Zahra, Muḥammad Abū. *Muhadarat fi'l-Nasraniyya* (1942, repr. Cairo: Dar al-Fikr al-Arabi, 1961.
Zakzouk, Mahmoud. *Einführung in den Islam*. Kairo: Ministerium für Religiöse Stiftungen, 2000.
Zebiri, Kate. *Muslims and Christians Face to Face*. Oxford: Oneworld, 1997.
Zeghal, Malika. "Religion and Politics in Egypt: The Ulema of al-Azhar, Radical Islam, and the State (1952-94)." *International Journal of Middle East Studies* 31 (1999): 371-399.
———. "The 'Recentering' of Religious Knowledge and Discourse: The Case of the al-Azhar in Twentieth-century Egypt." In *Schooling Islam: The Culture and Politics of Modern Muslim Education*. Edited by Robert W. Hefner and Muhammad Qasim Zaman. Princeton, NY: Princeton University Press, 2007, 107-130.

———. "Public Institutions of Religious Education in Egypt and Tunisia: Contrasting the Post-colonial Reforms of al-Azhar and the Zaytuna." In *Trajectories of Education in the Arab World: Legacies and Challenges*. Edited by Osama Abi Mershed. London: Routledge, 2009, 111-124.

———. "Cairo as Capital of Islamic Institutions? Al-Azhar Islamic University, the State and the City." In *Cairo Contested: Governance, Urban Space, and Global Modernity*. Edited by Diane Singerman. Cairo: The American University in Cairo Press, 2010, 63-81.

Beiträge zur Missionswissenschaft / Interkulturellen Theologie

Dieter Becker und Henning Wrogemann

Christel Ahrens; Ebise Ashana (Eds.)

In Memory of Them

150 years of Women Witnessing to Christ in Ethiopia (1868 – 2018)

The book presents accounts of women reformers in the Ethiopian Evangelical Church Mekane Yesus (EECMY). The editors collected their stories and put them in a historic context, covering a period of 150 years starting from the arrival of Gustava Lundahl from Sweden in 1870 with her vision of a girls' school. A large field of experiences is covered from slaves to high standing women; illiterate ones and Bible translators; teachers and medical professionals; women with family responsibilities and those, who dedicated their lives to the gospel; women who were imprisoned and those holding leading positions.

vol. 48, 2020, ca. 304 pp., ca. 34,90 €, br., ISBN-CH 978-3-643-91156-8

Josef Estermann

Befreiung oder Unterdrückung?

Mission und Theologie in der wechselvollen Geschichte von Kolonialismus und Dekolonisation

War die Missionstätigkeit der christlichen Kirchen im Verlaufe der Geschichte befreiend oder unterdrückend? Das vorliegende Buch gibt einen Überblick über die wechselvolle Geschichte des Christentums im Rahmen von Kolonialismus und Imperialismus. Es möchte Interessierte zu einer kritisch-konstruktiven Auseinandersetzung mit dieser historischen „Wahlverwandtschaft“ anregen, um zu einer „postkolonialen“ Theologie und Missionswissenschaft zu führen.

Bd. 47, 2019, 194 S., 29,90 €, br., ISBN 978-3-643-80313-9

Dirk Puder

Die Welt verändern

Transformatives Potential in Heilung und Mission der pentekostalen Religionsformation in den Entwürfen von Amos Yong, Veli-Matti Kärkkäinen und Opoku Onyinah

Die weltweit wachsende Pfingstbewegung hat eine neue Generation von Theologen und Theologinnen hervorgebracht, die die pentekostalen Erfahrungen im Lichte der gesamttheologischen Tradition erfasst und analysiert. Dadurch eröffnen sie Anschlüsse an die älteren Religionsformationen und vermitteln neue Impulse für ein zeitgemäßes, erfahrungsbezogenes theologisches Denken. Das Buch zeigt exemplarisch drei dieser Denkwege am Beispiel von göttlicher Heilung (Divine Healing) auf und analysiert sie im Lichte eines doxologischen Missionsverständnisses und neuerer kulturwissenschaftlicher Konzepte.

Bd. 46, 2020, ca. 272 S., ca. 34,90 €, br., ISBN 978-3-643-14481-2

John O'Brien

The QUR'AN and the CROSS

A study of al-Nisa (4):157. 'and they did not kill him and did not crucify him, but it was made to appear so to them'

vol. 45, 2020, ca. 264 pp., ca. 49,90 €, br., ISBN-CH 978-3-643-91082-0

Tobias Schuckert

Auf der Suche nach Verbundenheit

Der japanische Umgang mit der Tsunamikatastrophe 3.11 und eine Implikation der Theologie des Kuschelns

Bd. 44, 2018, 294 S., 39,90 €, br., ISBN 978-3-643-14222-1

Adolphus Chikezie Anuka

Mmanwu and Mission among the Igbo People of Nigeria

An Inculturative Dialogue

Bd. 43, 2018, 344 S., 34,90 €, br., ISBN 978-3-643-91063-9

LIT Verlag Berlin – Münster – Wien – Zürich – London

Auslieferung Deutschland / Österreich / Schweiz: siehe Impressumsseite

Muslim-Christian Relations (selected list)

Fadi Daou; Nayla Tabbara
L'hospitalité divine
L'autre dans le dialogue des théologies chrétienne et musulmane
« Cet ouvrage présente aux lecteurs un exposé sur la question de la diversité religieuse du point de vue croyant. Il a pour but de clarifier ce qu'avancent la foi chrétienne et la foi musulmane sur l'altérité religieuse. Son discours n'est pas élaboré pour l'autre, au risque d'édulcorer la vérité au profit de plus de sympathie, mais représente une construction théologique systématique s'adressant avant tout au croyant lui-même. Le défi face auquel ce livre met d'abord le croyant est celui d'accepter d'avancer vers l'autre muni, non d'une identit' religieuse figée comme d'une cuirasse, mais de la conviction que le message spirituel dont l'autre est porteur n'est peut-être pas étranger au plan de Dieu. »
(Cf. La préface du Prof. Jean Marc Aveline)
Colloquium salutis. Études en science et thélogie des religions, Bd. 1, 2. Aufl. 2014, 192 S., 24,90 €, br., ISBN-CH 978-3-643-90454-6

Fadi Daou; Nayla Tabbara
Göttliche Gastfreundschaft
Der Andere – Christliche und muslimische Theologien im Dialog. Übersetzt aus dem Französischen und mit einer Einführung von Uta Andrée, Werner Kahl und Harald Suermann
„Theologie ist dafür verantwortlich, getreu den eigenen Glaubenssätzen, eine Reflexion über den anderen und die Beziehung zu ihm anzustoßen." – Mit dieser Überzeugung treten die Islamwissenschaftlerin Nayla Tabbara und der katholische Theologe Fadi Daou aus dem Libanon in einen interreligiösen Dialog ein. Sie legen einander und ihren Lesern den Reichtum der Beziehungen zwischen Islam und Christentum dar und machen deutlich, wie stark der Gedanke des Bundes mit Gott beide Religionen trägt und sie miteinander verbindet. Sechs Kapitel voller Respekt und Offenheit für die Begegnung, die Gott selber als der freundliche Gastgeber ermöglicht. *Göttliche Gastfreundschaft* ist eine informative und inspirierende Einladung zum interreligiösen Dialog.
Theologie: Forschung und Wissenschaft, Bd. 54, 2017, 176 S., 24,90 €, br., ISBN 978-3-643-13278-9

Christoph Marcinkowski (Ed.)
The Islamic World and the West
Managing Religious and Cultural Identities in the Age of Globalization
Freiburger Sozialanthropologische Studien, vol. 24, 2009, 320 pp., 29,90 €, br., ISBN-CH 978-3-643-80001-5

Susanne Kurz; Claudia Preckel; Stefan Reichmuth (Hg.)
Muslim Bodies
Body, Sexuality and Medicine in Muslim Societies. Körper, Sexualität und Medizin in muslimischen Gesellschaften
Religionswissenschaft: Forschung und Wissenschaft, Bd. 14, 2016, 478 S., 59,90 €, br., ISBN 978-3-643-12810-2

Thomas Joseph Ndaluka
Religious Discourse, Social Cohesion and Conflict
Muslim – Christian Relations in Tanzania
Interreligious Studies, vol. 5, 2012, 288 pp., 24,90 €, br., ISBN-CH 978-3-643-90211-5

Kathrin Boukrayâa Trabelsi
Zwischen Bravo und Koran
Junge Muslima in Deutschland zwischen westlicher Moderne und religiöser Tradition
Jugend in Kirche und Gesellschaft, Bd. 11, 2015, 624 S., 64,90 €, br., ISBN 978-3-643-12999-4

Moritz Gräper
Jesus im Koran
Ein Beitrag zum christlich-muslimischen Gespräch
Interreligiöse Perspektiven, Bd. 7, 2014, 88 S., 24,90 €, br., ISBN 978-3-643-12759-4

LIT Verlag Berlin – Münster – Wien – Zürich – London
Auslieferung Deutschland / Österreich / Schweiz: siehe Impressumsseite